The Girl in the Mirror

Book 2

P. COSTA

THE GIRL IN THE MIRROR
BOOK 2

iUniverse books may be ordered through booksellers or by contacting:

iUniverse
1663 Liberty Drive
Bloomington, IN 47403
www.iuniverse.com
844-349-9409

ISBN: 978-1-6632-4194-8 (sc)
ISBN: 978-1-6632-4193-1 (e)

Library of Congress Control Number: 2022912814

Print information available on the last page.

iUniverse rev. date: 07/11/2022

To two good friends who are sisters to me. Pat and Pat prompted me to write down what was concerning me long ago. Thank you both for starting me on this journey.

And also to my Father in Heaven. He has poured out sources for good, prompting me to write these books.

California

As April watched the workers, she saw they had pulled onto a field full of rows of potatoes. They were laying on top of the ground, ready to be picked up into baskets. The workers were to fill the basket with potatoes and carry them back to a flatbed truck. It moved very slowly alongside the pickers so the workers wouldn't have to carry the full baskets very far.

April remembered that, back home, when she'd helped in the fields, she didn't have to bend over far. Her brothers called her "Shortie." April would fill one basket after another, but couldn't carry the full baskets to the flatbed truck. They were too heavy for her, so her brothers did that for her. The boss saw this and docked her wages. From dawn to dusk, they all worked. There were drink breaks and a lunch that lasted fifteen minutes. At the end of the day, April earned a check worth thirty-eight dollars. At five cents a basket, that meant she had filled 660 baskets of potatoes.

If April could have carried her baskets, then she would have made ten cents more each basket. But the truth was, April was too small to carry that heavy load. By day's end, she and everyone else were very tired and very dirty.

April remembered how proud she had been to hand the check to her Poppa, to prove to him she was worth something, that she could contribute to her family too. Poppa said nothing as he took all of their checks. He put them in a drawer in his desk and locked the drawer.

Mother took April into the bathroom and removed her clothing as dirt and stones fell to the floor. The dirt was on her hands, arms, and legs and in her hair. She had smudge marks on her face from sweating as she worked. Her shoes were filled with dirt, and her fingernails were torn and full of dirt. April's hands had many small cuts on them, and she sucked in her breath as she got into the tub of warm water. She held her hands in the water with her eyes closed tight.

Mother understood, because she knew how that felt. She didn't want to send her little girl into the field to pick onions, but that was her husband's idea. And April had done it. This little girl proved to her father that she was capable of doing anything asked of her, even if she was very young.

As April walked along, she realized this was a farming community. In the field, she saw all sorts of farming implements that she was familiar with. April turned and headed to a main street. There weren't too many buildings in this small town. It had a hardware store, a post office, a flower store, a small diner, and other stores like most small towns in America. April was tired and very hungry. She hadn't eaten in a long time. Her supplies were low, so she headed to the diner.

As she turned the doorknob and opened the door, a bell rang over her head. April entered and took a seat on a stool at the counter. She placed her things on the floor beside her.

"Hello there! Welcome. What can I bring for you?" said a very pretty woman.

"May I use the bathroom and then see a menu please?" April asked.

"Oh, shoot! There I go again. When it gets near the end of the day, I get sort of tired and think I'm at home. Ya know? Here ya go, sweetie." She laid a menu on the counter. "Sorry about that. Let me know what you'd like when you come out."

After April washed her hands, she came out of the ladies' room, then looked at the menu, and, in less than a minute, said, "May I please have a hot dog and an apple?"

"Oh, sure you can, and the apple is on me. Not too many young-uns like apples these days. They always want soda or candy."

The hot dog came out piping hot in a soft, buttery roll. April put on a small squeeze of mustard and took a big bite. "Yum." Just like she used to have at the Two Guys store with her mother. As you entered that store, there were Styrofoam heads with wigs on them, and right past that was the counter with the best hot dogs ever.

This hot dog was so good that April closed her eyes.

Then the woman said, "Well, I didn't know our hot dogs were that good," and she laughed.

April ate every bit of her hot dog, drank all of the free water, and pocketed her apple. Then she paid the woman fifty cents and left.

Whether her aunt was late or sick, or perhaps needed to find a way to pick her up, she would need somewhere to stay. She needed to find a safe place before dark.

As April walked, she stayed near the farming fields in the upper side of town. She passed five rows of homes.

As she passed each row, she noticed the farther she went, the older the homes became. At the last row, April saw what she was looking for. There was an older home, a Cape Cod, with a big front porch and a big backyard that hadn't been mowed in a long while. There were huge fields with migrant workers on the other side of the property. Along that wood line was April's new home.

Beside a tree was an old car, parked there a long time ago in that isolated place by the tree line. The car had once been black and shiny, but now all you could see were traces of black. It was mostly rusty, but the roof looked solid. April walked right up to the car. She didn't see anyone or hear anything other than dogs barking in the distance. She saw the car was very old. As she opened the passenger side door with several hard yanks, the door opened with a groan. April saw the floorboards were missing on the passenger side of the front seat. She looked around and saw a rusty radiator. She picked it up and pulled it into the car placing it where the floorboards were missing. She also found some old black mats with holes in them, but they fit pretty well to keep animals out of her new home.

April opened the back seat door, and to her surprise, the seat was whole, no springs sticking out, no holes. It didn't look too bad. And the car was quite cozy even though the back of the driver's seat had been removed. April put her backpack on the driver's seat so it would be easy to get it. April put her suitcase and tiger on either side of her.

The day was almost at an end, and it was almost dark. April stretched a little, covering herself with the small blanket Barbara had given to her, and soon she was asleep.

A raccoon that had lost his residence in the car scratched and scratched at that radiator.

April lay there, remembering to pray. Then she said her prayer. It was mostly a prayer of thanks for all the good people who had come into her life. She also asked for protection from harm and that the raccoon would stop scratching. Since the raccoon couldn't make the radiator move, he gave up and moved into the tree that towered above the old car.

And soon April was in a deep sleep.

The morning came, the air was thick and cloudy, and it was

still dark. April lifted her head ever so slightly to see if anyone could see her, but the area was quiet. She sat up, brushed her hair, smoothed out her clothing, and put another set of clothes in her bag. She opened the door slowly, so it wouldn't make a creaky noise. Carefully, quietly, she closed the door, and walked toward town.

April wasn't afraid. In time, she saw many friendly people. She waved hi, smiled, and kept walking, always keeping an eye out for her aunt.

April walked to the library that was open and busy. The big clock on the wall said it was nine o'clock. April was surprised she had slept so long. She pulled out a book that looked interesting. She held it in front of her, but she wasn't reading. She was watching people, trying to learn about the people in her new neighborhood.

One of the library aides came over to her and said, "You're early. The rest of the children will be arriving in about an hour. I'll come and get you for story time, though."

So they think I'm in the library program, coming to the library for story time, April thought.

Soon a big bunch of noisy children came spilling into the library. They followed a woman with a purple skirt who wore glasses. They all went to the back of the library, and up the stairs. April followed along behind. The children all sat on the floor on beanbag pillows, and a woman came to the front of the room with a book. She said her name, but April didn't remember it.

April was watching two boys who weren't listening, weren't behaving. As the woman read, the boys began to punch each other and other children. April looked around, and no one was paying attention to what the boys were doing.

April grabbed their shirt collars at the neck and said, "If you don't stop it, I'm going to karate chop you. Then you won't be able to breathe. You'll have a big red scar on your neck for the rest of your life."

The boys didn't expect that. They were afraid. Neither one said another word or moved until after the reading was over. Then they ran down the stairs to their mother who was waiting for them. All the children had mothers. April was the last child out of the room. The library clerk asked April where her mother was.

"She's working, ma'am. She's a nurse and works a lot." So there it was, her first lie. One she couldn't afford to forget.

April walked out of the library and headed to the town park. It was a lovely morning. She sat on the swing and stayed there swinging for several hours. Then she decided to walk around town and see her new neighborhood.

She took her time, her arms swinging at her side. April did want to stop somewhere to wash and change her clothing, but there was a whole day to fill.

April walked toward the grocery store in town. It was a busy day today. TUESDAY was the sign in large red letters on the entry door. April reasoned that must have something to do with all the old people in the store, and she was right. Tuesday was senior citizens' day, when the older people got a discount on their groceries—as much as ten percent. April walked around the store from aisle to aisle. This was a big store. It had many displays that were in the way of shopping carts as people came down the aisles. It was impossible for two carts to pass side-by-side. They had to maneuver around them.

At the very back of the store, April saw another sign. She wasn't good at reading, but she knew it was a bathroom because of the picture on the sign. April wasn't sure if she was allowed to go in. Just then the meat man came out with a large tray of meat to put in the display case. April pulled on his apron and asked him, "May I use the bathroom please?"

He looked at the little girl at his side. "Sure, you can. Just go through the door and walk a bit. There will be metal stairs on the left, go up the stairs, and the bathroom is at the top."

"Is it for boys and girls?" April asked.

"Well, it is, but you can lock the door when you go inside. There's a sliding lock," the meat man answered.

Off she went, pushing through the door, all the way back to the end of the store, up the metal stairs, and into the bathroom. April checked each stall to make sure there was no one in them, just her. Then she slid the metal lock in place. She began to run water, so it would get warm, and she undressed. April remembered to bring along a change of clothing in her backpack so she could put her dirty clothing in it after she was clean. April enjoyed the feeling of warm water and soap. It had been three days since she had been able to get clean. She washed every inch of her body.

Then she emptied the sink water, refilled it, and washed all over again, including her hair. She was enjoying the clean-head feeling when there came a knock on the door.

"Just a minute," April quickly said. "There is someone in here. I have diarrhea, and I can't open the door."

"Oh, okay," someone said on the other side of the door.

April stood still with the water dripping into the sink. She waited for a long time. When April felt satisfied that the person had left, she finished washing her hair. Next, she used her dirty shirt, turned inside out, for a towel to dry her hair. She dressed quickly into her clean clothing, socks, and shoes. Then she combed out her hair. She was all finished when there came another knock on the door. April reached up and slid the lock back. She stood back as an older woman entered the bathroom.

"You have been in here a long time, dear. Are you all right?" she asked April, looking at her as if through a magnifying glass.

"Yes. I feel much better. You see, I had diarrhea, and I couldn't get up to open the door. It's been going around in my family for days, and now I have it."

The woman's eyes opened wide, and she decided not to go in. April was upset that she'd done it again—she'd lied.

April knew she had to stop lying, but she didn't want to be found out. She prayed and asked God to forgive her. She felt God would, since she only lied to take care of herself. So long as she didn't hurt anyone else in any way, everything should be fine. April knew that her momma wouldn't be pleased with lying of any kind, but she also knew her momma taught her to be independent and responsible for herself and her actions.

Realizing her aunt wasn't coming, she had to make some difficult decisions. April wanted to go on with her life, but there was no one to help her. No one to give her advice, council, direction, or support. She was on her own.

So April rationalized that lying every once in a while wasn't too bad, but she would try her very best to keep lying at a minimum.

Soon April was outside again in the store parking lot, where she saw older ladies putting groceries in the trunk of their car. As they tried to close the trunk, the cart began to roll away. April quickly ran to grab the grocery cart and rolled it to the cart dock, which was a small open-sided shed building with a roof.

As April came back to pick up her bag, the older women called to her, "Little girl, little girl, come here."

April did, and the women dropped a quarter into the palm of her hand. April quickly learned a way for her to earn money. Time after time, April assisted older people, helping them unload their grocery bags or taking the carts to the cart dock. Each time, April received a quarter or dimes with nickels. One kind older man gave April a half dollar. She was very pleased with herself. She helped for an hour to earn money to buy her supper. April didn't want to spend much time at the store. She didn't want to be noticed or have the store manager chase her away. So she moved on.

April walked all around town. She saw a police cruiser go by. The man inside waved to her, and she waved back. April thought she should get some lunch, then go back to her home in the car. As she began to walk toward her home, she saw an old man on the sidewalk. He was surveying the house and looking from side to side. Finally, he went into the garage that was to the left side of the house. April felt the getting was good, so she ran as fast as she could to the car. She stood there for a minute, to make sure no one would see her, and then she got in.

"Phew," she said, "I made it." She hoped getting home wouldn't always be as exhausting, and a rush, as it was this time. As April sat there, very still, she could hear neighbors mowing grass, some whistling to dogs, dogs barking, and music—all sorts of different kinds. And soon she was asleep for a much-needed nap.

She awoke with a start. There was a dog outside by the car, and he was barking. A man was calling to him, "Barkley, Barkley, come back here. You big dummy, let that raccoon alone." The man came close to the car when Barkley decided to run to his owner.

"I have to get out of here," April said to herself. She left the car and looked around. The coast was clear. April walked briskly through town and headed to the diner and that bell on its door.

She was hungry. As she entered the diner, the bell rang. The lady looked up and said, "Oh. It's you again, sweet pea. Come on in." This time April walked to the back of the room and sat at a table.

The lady came over. "Honey, you and I need to be better acquainted." She reached out to shake her hand, and said, "My name is Flo, short for Florence," with a big smile on her face.

April shook her hand. "My name is April. My momma is a nurse and works a lot. I'm here for dinner."

Flo was shocked. Who would leave such a little girl on her own?

It was as if April could read her thoughts. So she said, "My momma taught me to be safe. She said this was a safe place with good homemade food. That's why she moved to this town and why she allows me to come here."

Flo had been reprimanded, and soon April was sitting with a stuffed pepper and a glass of milk. She finished her supper, dabbing her face with a napkin. She slid off of her chair and went to the counter to pay for her supper.

"That will be eighty-five cents," said Flo.

April handed her a dollar, and said, "Keep the change. Okay?"

April went out the door. She didn't like when people doubted her or when they assumed things about her. She could take care of herself—she was smart. She headed back to her car before nightfall. She didn't want to be outside in the dark.

April was very sleepy, but she remembered that she and her momma prayed every night before she went to bed. So she got down on her knees with her head on the back seat and began.

"Dear God, please watch over me. Keep me safe and out of trouble. Please watch over my family so many bus stops away. Watch over us and keep us safe. Don't let any of us get into trouble. We sometimes do, and that makes Poppa very mad. But since I'm here, I don't have to worry about Poppa. I'm trying to be brave and behave myself like my brothers told me to. And I try not to cry."

Then her tears began to roll down her cheeks. "It's just that sometimes I feel so all alone. Even though I have made some friends. Each night I come to this place, my home. It's not like it used to be when I was scared. I used to go to someone's bed and crawl in."

She took a big breath. Then she shuddered. "I'm trying so very, very hard to be good, be brave, and help others. I'll try harder to be strong. Please be with me, God, and help me. Please, in Jesus Christ's name. Amen."

Sleep came easily. It had been a good day. April wanted to make a daily routine and learn who the people were. After a while, it should come easier to her.

George

Morning came early. April was awake by four o'clock, before anyone else. She did see one car drive down the street, but she was the only one up—well, her and the raccoon. April got used to seeing him and shared leftover food. He came down, rubbed it, and then ate. April didn't get close to the raccoon because she knew better. Soon she was off to explore. She followed her usual routine. She saw the workers in the fields coming in trucks. They got out and began to pick again.

April arrived at the far end of town. The clock outside on the building said it was 7:00 a.m., but the minute hand wasn't moving. This was a garage, but it looked like it was out of business. There were large containers standing up in the parking lot that were full of junk. Many had old cans and broken glass in them. There were weeds hanging all around April's head. The place looked messy, so April began to put the cans in one large container and glass in another. Soon she found a hand scythe hanging on a nail on the outside of the building. She picked it off the nail and began to cut grass—one handful after another. In no time, she was sweating and making good progress. April kept swinging that scythe, and soon she noticed the shadow of a man in front of her.

April looked up squinting her eyes in the bright sunshine, and the man asked. "What are you doing here?"

"Well, what does it look like?" April said as she wiped the sweat from her brow.

The man said, "Looks like you're making a mess."

"Are you kidding me?" replied April, "I'm making this mess better, and you know it."

The man shuffled his feet. His sneakers were dirty and very worn. He pulled April up to a standing position and shook her hand. "Hi, I'm George. Well, George Jr., and this is my garage. I got it from my pop, but he's not with me anymore, though."

April looked at George. "Hello, George, I hope you don't mind, but you need some help."

George laughed at her. "Well, you're right about that."

So, short stuff, are you looking for a job?"

"If you're offering, I'll take it," April replied, and they both laughed.

"Come on inside," George said. April did, and the garage inside was in worse condition than the outside. She didn't know where to sit. She pulled some books off a stool and sat down. George came out with two ice-cold Coca-Colas in his hands.

"You thirsty?" asked George.

"You bet," April replied, and they both sat there enjoying the icy cold Cokes. They let the burps come out, and laughed at each other.

George Jr. was a very laidback man. He was greasy all over. He had grease on his pants, T-shirt, shoes, and his face. He had thick black wavy hair and the shadow of a beard that didn't leave his face. April liked George instantly.

George was sitting with his eyes closed. It didn't seem like any customers were coming in today or anytime soon.

April was sure that she had seen something like this before. It happened to a neighbor who didn't work and slept a lot. Her husband died in a car crash, and she wasn't interested in anything. In time, that woman became useless, and her home became trashed. The doctor removed her from her home, and April never saw her again.

As April stared at George, she was determined to whip him into shape, and the sooner, the better.

"Hey, well, George. I had a nice time drinking your soda, but I'm going to go. I want to get something to eat at the diner. If you want to come along, you can. I'm going to come back tomorrow and work here, if that is okay with you?" April said.

"That's fine," said George, still sitting in his chair with his eyes closed. So she hopped off of the books and headed to Flo's.

April came in and listened for that bell. Then she walked to the back of the diner and sat down.

As Flo came out of the kitchen, April said, "Hi, Flo," and Flo was surprised. Flo came with a menu, and April said, "I'll just have a cheeseburger and some applesauce. If that's okay?"

"Sure thing," said Flo. "Coming right up."

April saw several people in the diner, and at the counter was the man in the uniform who always waved to her. The man was speaking to Flo, "Flo, who is that beautiful young girl sitting over there?"

"Why that's April, Sheriff."

The sheriff got off of his stool. He was a very handsome man, tall and fine. He had very little hair showing out of his hat. He wore a crisp uniform, complete with a holster and gun. He came over to April and introduced himself.

"Hello, April, my name is Sheriff Di Angelo. It's a pleasure to meet you."

"Same here," answered April.

"Do you live around here, miss?" the sheriff asked.

"I do, sir, but my momma is a nurse and works a lot. I'm never in trouble. I do work and try to keep busy and stay out of trouble," said April.

"I just knew you were special," the sheriff said. "How I wish everyone tried as hard as you do. Then this world would be a much happier place. I must go now, but you enjoy your meal." And with that, the sheriff was gone.

April ate her meal, and when she went to pay, Flo said to her, "It's all taken care of, darling. The sheriff paid your bill when he left."

April didn't waste any time, so she hurried and watched for a safe time to crawl into the car. She prayed and fell asleep while she was still on her knees. She never got up. She covered up with the small blanket and didn't hear anything.

April awoke, not sure what time it was, but it was still dark outside. She wanted to leave early to get a good start on the garage. By the time George came in the office, his eyes widened.

"Holy cow! What did you do?" he asked.

"Cleaned it," answered April.

George ran his hand over the counter and tables. "Nice, very nice, short stuff. If you keep this up, I'll be back in business in no time."

"I hope so," April said.

George looked around, and all the books were clean and in order, the windows were clean, and the sun shined through them. Everything was clean and bright.

"George, will you help me clean the garage area?" asked April.

"Okay, I will. Do you want to do that now?" George asked her.

"Sure," April said, and so they began. It took them until dark to do such a huge job, but everything was done. The walls, tools, and lines were all clean. Everything was hung where it belonged. All that was left to do was the garage floor and pit areas.

"Hey, short stuff, let's knock off now," George said.

"We did a good job. Let's go and get something to eat."

George walked to a big black pickup truck, opened his door, and got in. He looked down, and there stood April.

"Where are we going, and when are we coming back? I'm not allowed to be out too late past dark," she said.

"Well, we can go to Fresno to a nice pizza place, and I promise to take you home—right to your door. Okay?" asked George.

"Well, I guess it's okay," April, said and she stood there.

George asked her why she wasn't getting in. April told him that she needed the door opened and help to get in. George laughed, opened the passenger side door, and helped April into his truck.

April said, "You may as well get used to it, George. You will have to open your door on dates and when you're married too." They were off and on their way in the loudest sounding truck April had ever ridden in.

The pizza place was really nice. They had all sorts of pizzas, not just pizza like she was used to. George liked the meat pizza, and she like it too. But she also liked the vegetable pizza—so they got half and half. George got a beer, and April got a Sprite soda. April saw the clock and began to eat in a hurry.

"Short stuff, slow down. You are going to choke," George said.

April looked at George and said, "Okay, but my name is April. Please stop calling me short stuff. Okay? I must be home very soon, and you know that. I told you."

George smiled. "Stop sweating the small stuff, April. I'll have you home in ten minutes."

They finished eating, and George Jr. paid the bill. Then they went out to his truck and raced home.

George dropped April in front of the little house. He wanted to wait until she went inside, but April just stood there waiting for him to leave, so he did. His truck pipes went blasting diesel fuel into the sky. The old man looked out of his curtains, and April ducked down by the hedge not to be seen. April walked in the dark to the car and hopped in. She noticed the house lights where the man lived went out. It was 8:00 p.m.

The House

She thought about the day. It had been a good day. She loved to help people and got a good feeling inside from helping.

April was so tired that as soon as she began her prayers, her thoughts were lost in the webs of sleep.

There were strange noises that disturbed her sleep. She heard an owl screech, and there was scratching on the bottom of the car. But nothing got her fully awake. April slept through until 5:00 a.m. the next morning.

In the morning, April looked at the little house, and the lights were on. As she watched, the little old man went to his garage and drove away. This was her chance. April opened the car door, then closed it, and raced to the back of the little house.

She was standing at the basement cellar doors. She pulled open one side and stepped down the steps, letting the metal door close. She went to the wooden door in front of the bottom step and turned the knob. It opened.

This was a basement cellar. It was dark, but soon, April's eyes adjusted to the light. She saw there was food storage—it was handier to go downstairs instead of driving into town. There were all sorts of canned goods, ketchup, mustard, and cleaning supplies.

As she walked through the basement, there was a small bathroom on the right after the pantry. It also had a small window to the right side of the house. Beyond that was a washer and dryer, and at the end of that wall was a stairway that led upstairs to the first level of the house.

All along the stairwell bottom, there were coats hung on hangers, women's coats with fur collars. And there were boxes, lots of boxes filled with something. The name *Elaine* was on each box. April wasn't sure what was in them, so she sounded out the words: shirts, dresses. April wasn't sure who Elaine was or why all of her clothing was down in the basement. Suddenly April stood very still, something had touched her leg. Then she heard, "Meow." April looked down, and there was a big orange tabby cat with his tail touching April's legs.

"Hello. What's your name?" April said as she stroked the cats head and back.

"Meow," said the cat. He was happy for the attention.

April looked around, and then she went up the stairs to the first level of the house. It was a small house. She entered the kitchen. A kitchen table and two chairs were in the center of the room, to the right a sink and cupboards, to the left was a refrigerator. There were some pictures hanging up on the walls, and some pots with dried dead flowers sitting in the windows.

April went to her far left and discovered a small parlor or sitting room. In this room there was a television. It was a very old black-and-white model. It had rabbit-ear antennas on the top of it. The room also had two small recliner rocker chairs with small rugs where feet would go.

Each had a small table beside the rocking chairs with cups, glasses, and reading material. There were no windows in this room. There was a large metal box that must have been used for heat, but it was cold and no longer used.

That room led to another set of stairs that went up to the second floor that April wanted to see. There were three other rooms upstairs: a bathroom and two bedrooms. One bedroom was still being used. The bed was unmade, and there were clothes hung on a chair and on the bottom bed rail. There were shoes under a dresser and slippers at the bedside.

The table beside the bed had a picture of a very pretty woman. April didn't know who that was, so she kept going.

The second bedroom was empty except for a few boxes. Those too had the name *Elaine* written on them.

April went back downstairs and opened the refrigerator. Oh, there was food, lovely cooked food, a chicken, meatloaf, and other things that she liked to eat.

She thought it would be all right for her to take just a little bit of food. She got a paper plate. There was a stack of them beside the microwave, and she made sure to use a napkin. She made a small plate with a bit of everything and put it in the microwave. She turned the knob to one minute to heat up her food. When the minute was over, the microwave dinged, signaling it was done. Now her family didn't have one of these ovens, but Barbara did, and that is how April had learned to use one.

April took out her food and smelled it. "Ah!" She missed her momma's cooking, and this reminded her. April didn't sit down. She stood and ate her small sampling of food and kept the paper plate with her.

She went back down into the basement. That's when she heard a car, and she peeked out of the basement bathroom window. She saw the old man coming out of his garage. April was afraid to be seen, so she hid herself in the clothing along the wall that was hanging up. The old man came in the front door, and banged it closed. Then he called a name.

"Arnold. Come here, Arnold." The sound of a can opening got the cat's attention, and he scampered up the stairs. April heard something being put into a dish, and the man set the dish on the floor.

"There you go, now. Don't be begging me for food," he said. April was very still. She could hear her heart beating. Soon the upstairs basement door was closed, and she could hear that the television was on.

A Job

THIS WAS HER CHANCE TO get out, and she did, ever so carefully and quietly. April headed into town to see what George Jr. was doing. Surprisingly, when April arrived at the garage, there was George, sweeping the pit out. April stood at the crevasse and looked down at him, "Everything all right?" she asked.

"Good as it can get," replied George. "I'll be up when I'm finished."

"Okay. I'm going into the office," April said, and she did.

The office was in need of something, but she couldn't put her finger on it. April sat there on the stool, and all of a sudden, the telephone rang very loudly. On the second ring, April picked up the phone and tried to sound like a grown-up.

"Hello, George's garage."

"Hey, is George there?" the voice asked.

"No, he's busy at the moment. May I help you?" she asked the voice.

"Well, maybe. Hey, yeah. Ask George when I can come in and have him look at my radiator. It's leaking again," the voice said.

"Will you hold on a moment?" April asked.

"Yeah, yeah, I'll hold," the voice replied.

April scooted off of the stool and ran to the pit.

"George, someone wants you to look at their radiator. When can they come in, and how long will that take?" she asked.

George came up out of the pit and went to the phone. "Hey, this is George."

"George, this is Ray Fluck. I have that same radiator problem again, and I was hoping I could bring the truck in for you to look at it. It will soon be produce time again, and I don't need this problem."

George looked for his schedule book, but couldn't see it.

"Ah, bring it in tomorrow about ten o'clock. Okay?" said George as he scribbled the time and date down on a cover of a book, along with the customer's name.

"Okay, George. I sure appreciate it. See you tomorrow at ten o'clock," and they both hung up their phones.

"April, did you see a blue book with big blocks in it, sort of like a calendar?"

"This?" April held up a book that was laying on the counter right beside the telephone.

"Yup, that's it," said George. He looked at her and then said, "Come here. I want to show you how to do this." He turned to the date in the book, and to the ten o'clock time slot. Then he flipped the book to the front cover, and there it showed approximate times that it took to do certain jobs give or take.

George showed her how to block the time off. April looked at George and said, "I can't read so well."

George laughed and said, "Neither can I. All you need to do is put down a letter," and he showed April how to do this two or three times until April understood.

Throughout the day, cars would drive by slowly and see the two of them outside raking the lot or just moving tires. And soon the phone would ring with someone needing an appointment. April would run to the phone and answer it. "Hello, George's Garage. How may I help you?" and the voice on the other end would say when they wanted to come in, or April would suggest a time. She would put in their last name, they always had to spell it. Then she would hang up the phone with the block of time marked in the front of the scheduling book. In less than two weeks, George's business took off, and he said it was like old times with his pop.

During this time April and George had a lot of meals at the diner. Flo would hover over them. She was delighted at the positive changes in George. His father had died unexpectedly of a heart attack while working outside at the garage.

Sometimes during their lunch or dinner visit at the diner, Flo's son would come and sit by George. His name was Brad, and he was Flo's one and only child. He had no father and often was in trouble. Brad was a lone wolf. He didn't have many friends, and those who were his friends weren't good examples—always drinking alcohol and driving around. Flo would wring her hands and try to talk to Brad, but he never wanted to hear her. He was a man now, and he had his own life to live.

When Brad was disrespectful to Flo in front of George or April, both of them would remind Brad not to talk like that. In time, Brad got the picture, and he began to change toward Flo. One day while sitting in the garage office, April asked George, "George, don't you think you need help in the garage?"

"Well," said George, "it would be nice if work was consistent, but we aren't busy every day."

"What about part-time?" April asked.

"That would be great, but who wants a part-time job?" George answered her.

"They may not know they want it, but I think that Brad would be good working with you. You could teach him a lot," April said.

"Well, I'm not much of a teacher, and it would take me twice as long to get a job done," George said almost with a whine.

"Yes, it would," April replied. "But not all the time. After two or three times, he'd get it. And you wouldn't need to show him again. And in time, he would take a lot of work off of your load."

"Ah, maybe," said George. "Maybe."

April wasn't a *maybe* girl. When things needed to be done, she was one to pull up her sleeves and get it done. So one day she was sitting outside on the bench in front of the diner, and Brad came to sit beside her.

"How are you, April?" he said squeezing her arm.

"I'm okay, but I have a problem?"

"You do?" Brad said, interested.

"Yes, you see George has too much work sometimes at the garage, and no one wants to bend wrenches or get dirty. It's only once in a while that things get crazy busy, but when they do, I wish there was someone who wanted to learn to be a great mechanic like George."

"Shoot, I'd do it," said Brad.

"Really?" April said with a smile. "How about you come by tomorrow about eleven o'clock, and George will talk to you? How's that?"

"Oh, awesome," said Brad, and he tousled her hair.

Brad thought he had just gotten the best of April, but he didn't know April, and she had a plan. April squeezed her legs and entire body together with the thought of Brad working, learning. And besides, Flo would be so pleased.

So that Thursday, a little before eleven o'clock, in walked Brad. George was swamped with oil changes and a car on the lift.

"Need some help, George?" Brad asked.

"Uh, do you know how to put oil in a car?" asked George.

Brad looked at him, smiling, answering him, "Duh." And he did that job for George.

The customers thanked Brad and gave him tips—sometimes as much as five dollars. Then the customers would go into the office to pay their bill. The bill fee was simple—a different charge for different things, with most charges being ten to twenty-five dollars. George said he and Pop kept the prices low so more customers would come in. "You'll never be rich, but you'll always have good-paying customers."

That's how Brad became a mechanic working beside George. As time went on, Brad showed his interest and intelligence. He was very adept with cars and trucks. He liked working on them and figuring out their problems.

The two men took breaks together and talked about the jobs and how they solved the problems. Sometimes, they would talk about weekend plans. They got along well, and it was a pleasant working place for all.

One day while April was there with George, Brad was sent out to pick up lunch. April said to George, "It's so nice having Brad help out. It is not every day, but when it's busy, Brad sure has been a big help to you."

George looked at her and winked. "Yep, I sure was smart on that one."

April threw a work rag at him, and they both laughed.

April knew she couldn't stay at the garage and help out. Number one, she was underage. Number two, she didn't want to bring attention to herself. Number three, George needed to find someone to work there, and he was such a stick-in-the-mud guy. So again, April had to make a plan.

Matchmaking

IT HAD BEEN THREE MONTHS now living in Carruthers. April got to know many of the people by first and last name. April made a routine of going to the library twice a week, always remembering to return her books. She ate at the diner for lunch, and sometimes George picked up dinner. She often went to the Piggley Wiggley for a hot dog or a sub sandwich. April went swimming on hot days at the invitation of friends, and she even found a church that she liked to go to on Sundays.

April wasn't sure what kind of church it was, but she liked it. There were no statues, everyone was friendly, and there were no priests or pastors. People would go up front to the podium and give talks. Most were very interesting to April, but sometimes she would fall asleep. There was a sacrament meeting, then Sunday school, and lastly primary.

April loved to sing songs about Jesus and tried to obey her teachers. Sometimes, kids would tease April. It wasn't nice. They said she was bad and didn't have a mom or dad.

"I do too," April would say. Then the teacher would bend down and talk with her. Sometimes, that would make April cry. She was doing nothing wrong, and she got the talking to—not a mean talk, but a talking to of love and care. Usually, she was hugged, and that made her feel that everything was all right.

So one day, when George was finishing up on a job, April stopped by the garage. George said, "Hey, there, I haven't seen you in a while. Where have you been?"

"Oh, here and there," replied April.

George said, "I stopped by your house, but an old man said he lived there. Did you move?"

April froze. "No. No, we didn't move. I don't live in that house. I live a couple of houses up the street. I only stopped there, so you wouldn't wake up Mom with your loud truck."

"Oh," said George, "I was just a little worried."

"Miss me, eh?" April teased, and George came after her, picking her up as she began to giggle. April loved George, but what he said next frightened her.

"I'd like to meet your mom," George said. "Maybe she and I could hook up. You know, go dating."

April replied sarcastically, "Yeah, for real, pfft! My mom is almost forty and you want to date her. Yuk!"

George quickly recovered and said, "I didn't know," and never mentioned that again.

Church

APRIL AND GEORGE HIT IT off and began a friendship that would last a lifetime. He was like a big brother, and she was his little sister. They could talk all day or say nothing. And they got along just fine.

April wanted to ask George one of the biggest questions she had inside her. One day, she built up the courage to ask if she could tell him.

"Sure, you can ask me anything. I won't yell at you or nothing. You know that!" he said.

April took a deep breath and, looking directly at George, said, "George, will you go to church with me?"

George stared at her. "Why?"

"Because I want you there with me," was her reply.

"Does it mean that much to you?" asked George.

"Yes, yes, it does," said April. "I go alone, and I sit alone. I have no one to talk to. It's only on a Sunday. Please, will you go with me?"

George would do just about anything for her. She had helped him when he didn't know he needed help. "Sure, I'll go along with you—where and what time?"

"This Sunday at 8:45 a.m. I'll meet you here."

And that was that.

The following Sunday, true to her word, and George never doubted her, April was standing in front of the garage driveway. George got out of his truck dressed in a blue suit and white shirt, trying to tie his tie.

"Wow! You look nice," April hollered.

George smiled. She sure had a way with compliments, and she sure had a way of talking a person into doing things that they weren't one hundred percent convinced on doing. George laughed to himself.

They arrived at the church a few minutes early. The parking lot was full, but George had plenty of room to park his oversize diesel truck. George got out and opened the passenger side door to help April out. She was wearing a dress, and George wanted to help April out discreetly. As they walked together toward the building, there was a sign that George stopped to read *The Church of Jesus Christ of Latter-Day Saints.* George didn't know what it was or what kind of church, he just followed close behind April into the chapel.

As they entered the building, there were young men handing out programs. They smiled at George and April and said, "Welcome."

As they continued into the building, it was impossible to keep to themselves. People walked up to them and extended their hands to shake, saying, "My name is so-and-so." In all his life attending church, which wasn't much, George had never been recognized and welcomed like that.

They soon went into the chapel and found a seat in a pew. The pews were filling up fast with families, some with children, and older couples too. Before long, a man who was sitting at the front of the chapel stood up at the podium and announced the opening song. The page number of the song was also on the side wall. April leaned forward and picked up a hymnal. George helped her find the page, and the two of them began to sing the hymn.

Goodness, George had a nice singing voice. April was so

impressed that she couldn't keep from looking at him instead of trying to follow the words on the page.

After the hymn, someone walked up front for the opening prayer. He gave such a lovely prayer—heartfelt and thoughtful. Then he sat down in his seat. He was followed by young men carrying trays of bread for everyone in the rows—for people to take and eat. This represented Jesus's body. After that, the young men brought trays of water in cups, which represented the blood of Jesus Christ. It was for them to commit to Jesus, to always remember him, and keep his commandments. April loved that idea, and she did try very hard to do all of that, every day.

Then the first speaker came forward to the podium. She spoke about being there for someone. It was a good talk. April agreed that it was nice to help someone and be there for them. You never knew if and when you might need help.

George was listening too, but he was also looking around, particularly at some of the young women. April elbowed George in his side.

"Umph," George groaned quietly. He gave April a look and continued what he was doing before. After sacrament was Sunday school. April went to a class of young children her age. George was taken into another room where there were adults studying the Old Testament of the Bible. After that was a men's class for George and a primary class for April.

George was stopped in the hallway by a customer who had his vehicle at George's garage. They both chatted for a while. The man's daughter was with him. She was in her twenties and very, very pretty. Her name was Katie.

After all classes were over, April came into the hallway to see

George talking to Katie. She didn't know they had met earlier here. April kept her distance. She didn't want to interrupt them while they were talking together. Soon George took Katie's hand and shook it, and he looked around for April. When he saw her, he motioned for her to come to him. She did.

"Are you ready to get out of here?" he asked. April nodded yes. Outside, George told April he had been invited out to dinner and asked if April wanted to go along.

"Oh no. That's all right," April said. "You go on, and have a nice time. I should go home and see Momma before she leaves for work again." April wasn't sad. She was happy for George. He always kept to himself, and now he had been invited out. Besides, she had a secret to guard. It was best that she head on home.

The Sheriff

On her way home, April saw the sheriff's car. It was sitting in front of the post office. There was no one in the car. April crossed the street and was so surprised that the police station was right beside the post office. She had never noticed that before because there was a big hanging basket in the window. It had vines that went back and forth, crisscrossing the window and leaving little room to read the sign.

As April walked by slowly, the sheriff came outside. He put his hat on and adjusted it when he noticed April.

"Hello, April. How are you today on this beautiful Sunday?"

"I'm good," April said and kept walking fast. She liked the sheriff a lot, but she knew from living with her family not to be too friendly with the police.

"Hold on there a minute," the sheriff said. "Are you in a hurry to go somewhere?"

"Well. Yes, I am," said April and kicked the sidewalk as she walked. Dang, she'd done it again—another lie.

"Well, lookie here," the sheriff said. "Would you like to come inside, and see our police station?"

"Oh, I'd like to, very much, but you see I must be going. I have dawdled enough. I have to go," April said.

"Okay then, it's too bad because my wife made really good cheesecake cruller doughnuts with lots of apricot jelly on them," the sheriff said.

April was a sucker for sweets, and she was always hungry. She slowed down and turned around. Then she looked at him directly in his eyes while turning her head sideways.

"Doughnut and that's all?" she said.

"Doughnut and that's it," the sheriff said, laughing.

April went up two steps to enter the police station, and the sheriff held the door open for her. It was a nice big office with three big rooms for other policemen to work in. In the very back were the cells. That made April shudder. She didn't want to see them. It wasn't a fancy place. It had a lot of maps on the wall and telephones on each desk. April was drawn to the maps, and stood there staring at them.

"You like maps?" the sheriff asked.

"I do, but, well, I was wondering where we are on that map," April said.

"Well, if you look right here." The sheriff held a pencil in his hand, circling the area. "This here is Carruthers, and over here is Fresno, which you can see is much bigger."

April looked, and she did see. The sheriff saw what he yearned for. He saw a beautiful little girl with the brightest eyes he had ever seen and rosy cheeks. Also, she was polite and so darned determined to have her own way. She reminded him so much of his wife. His heart leaped each time he saw this little girl. He wondered where her father was, that she was allowed to roam the streets so often. But he knew better than to ask. This was a doughnut date, nothing more. He knew he would have to earn her trust. She was like a wild filly—she would come to eat, but don't try to catch her. No, no. She would come on her own when she was good and ready.

"How about sitting down here and pick out your doughnut? But I have to tell you I think they're all good."

April followed him to a table and sat up on the chair he provided.

He also got a large phone book for her to sit on to boost her closer. April's eyes grew wide with anticipation, and her tummy growled.

"Let me help you a bit," the sheriff said, and he slid a sticky cream cheese with peach jelly cruller onto the paper plate in front of her.

April leaned over to smell it. Instantly, she was whirled back home where her momma baked delicious treats. She didn't give way to tears but sat there with her eyes closed remembering.

The sheriff waited patiently. He thought April was praying. And when she looked up, he had a fork dangling in front of her.

"You'll need this," he said. "They are soft and sticky." True to his word, they were, but he forgot to add *delicious*. As they ate, the sheriff asked April what she liked to do. April didn't take much time when she looked up at him, answering. "Well, mostly I like helping people. But, pretty close to that, I like riding horses."

"You don't say," said the sheriff excitedly. "Well, I like horses too. In fact, I have five of them right now, and a couple of ponies too."

"What do you have them for?" April asked with her mouthful.

"Well, I like horses and ponies, but I like to make money too. So when I find someone looking for a nice, well-cared-for and trained horse or pony, then I sell them," answered the sheriff.

April remembered her momma doing that very same thing, and April was beginning to warm up to the sheriff. She reasoned he couldn't be so mean if he had horses and ponies. They take a lot of time and patience.

She sat there chewing on her cruller, and the sheriff asked her if she wanted something to drink. April nodded yes. The sheriff got up, crossed the floor to his office, and brought out a container of milk.

"The guys use this in their coffee," he said, and he poured April a half glass of milk.

April took the glass and swallowed deeply. The milk was cold and good. "Ahh, thank you so much," she said. "It is so good and cold."

The sheriff's eyes smiled at her as he nodded in agreement.

All too soon, their little snack session ended, and April asked to wash her hands. Then she had to go. The sheriff held the door open for her to wash up. Meanwhile, another policeman came in with a report.

"The Browns' cow is down in the bog again. They called us earlier, and I went out and saw it. She's in pretty deep, so it seems."

The sheriff held the door for April. She came out, and he said, "April, I must go out on a call, so if you want to go, you may."

April looked at him. And then she said, "I would rather go with you on the call to help the cow out," and the two officers laughed.

So there she sat in the squad car with the sheriff, while the other officer got George with his come-along. Then the officer rode with George. They drove out to the countryside, and as they went along, there was squelching and sounds coming out of the radio in the sheriff's car.

"That's our CB radio. It tells us where there is trouble or someone needing help." As they rode over a crest of a hill, the sheriff pointed to the right. "See over there? That's where I live."

April looked and saw a white farmhouse with several barns or outbuildings around it. She saw horses in a field that went way out over a hill to the woods.

"It's a nice place," April said, and they continued on.

Within minutes, they arrived at the Browns' farm. George backed his rollback with the winch into the driveway all the way to the back of the barn. April and the sheriff walked in front of the truck guiding it. At the back of the barn, Mr. Brown opened the gate to the pasture, and in the distance, they could hear the cow mooing. She had bogged down in the soft end by the creek. The officer took the winch and began to walk with it as far as he could go. As he ran out of line, George would back up the truck. Finally, they reached the bogged-down cow and the mud. The officer signaled for the truck to stop. When the sheriff saw the signal, he hollered George to stop.

They all approached the cow, trying to figure out what would be the best way to get her up and out.

Then April said, "Roll her over. Then she can get up on her own."

They thought she was kidding, but she tugged on the sleeve of the sheriff and said it again.

"How are we supposed to roll her over when she's stuck?" he asked April.

"She's not that stuck." April walked in the mud and took hold of the cow's back leg trying to turn it. Soon all the men were helping her. They pulled the cow's leg over to one side. Then all of a sudden, the cow lurched up, stood, and walked away toward the herd.

Everyone began to laugh. Mr. Brown wanted to know how April knew how to do that trick.

She said, "I grew up on a farm, and we had cows do that too," and she turned to go. She washed her hands at the pump and rinsed her shoes. Her socks weren't saved, but there was nothing to be done about them. She walked to the sheriff's car, and waited. They all came up to the barn to wash the mud from their shoes and hands and began to leave. The sheriff came over to the passenger side, opening the door for April to get in.

April hopped inside, and the sheriff got in. Before he started the cruiser, he turned to her and said, "You sure kept us out of a big job, and I want to thank you."

"Oh, that's all right. I like helping." April wiggled a bit in the seat. She was beginning to really like this sheriff and didn't want him to know—not yet. She had to be safe. She had to protect herself, so the ride home was very quiet.

"Is there anywhere you want to go, April?" the sheriff asked. "To your house or somewhere?"

"No, I just want to go back, maybe to the park. You see, Momma has a long shift today."

So as he drove back to Carruthers, his mind began to whirl. How he wished this little girl were his and his wife's.

There was a lot of potential to this little one. And he knew his wife and he would love the chance to help her, if they were allowed.

Back in town, April quickly opened the car door, and waved to him saying, "Thanks." And she was off.

The sheriff just sat there feeling as if he were stood up for a date. There were so many things he wanted to say to her, but he felt her put up a wall.

Like all women, there was no sense pressing them. Let them alone, and they'd come around. That was his theory. In time, his theory would prove him right.

The Injury

April headed to the park, looking over her shoulder from time to time. But no one followed her. She sat on the big swings under the canopy of the trees and began to swing. Getting momentum, going higher and higher, she giggled at the feeling. From this height she could see very far. But she couldn't see her home. She knew that she was far from where she lived with her family. That bus ride had been very long.

There was no aunt, for sure. If she dwelled on being alone, she became very frightened. She knew, if she just listened and did what she knew was right, then she would be okay. As she slowed down on the swing, she jumped and fell. She felt something sharp in her hand. She stood still, opening her hand as big as it would go, and there was a large piece of glass in her palm.

April didn't know how to get that glass out, so she headed to George's garage. George was there cleaning up the rollback to put it away inside his garage. He was ready to close for the day. The workload had been a light one, and it was Friday night. He'd made plans with someone special, but in walked April.

"George, I have a problem," she said, holding her hand out for him to see.

"Oh geez. That's nasty," said George, looking at the glass in her hand.

"Can you take it out, George?" April asked.

"Well, I can try, but I can't say for sure if I can get the whole thing. That's a big, nasty piece of glass. Where did you get it?" George asked.

"At the park swing," April answered.

George had gotten out a needle and begun to light a lighter to sterilize it when Katie pulled up.

"Hey, everyone," she said.

"Hey," said George, "Will you come over here and look at this?"

Katie did, and she made a face. "That's pretty bad. Maybe she should go to the emergency room to have that removed, and maybe she should get a tetanus shot. Do you know if you ever had a tetanus shot, April," Katie asked.

April shook her head no.

"Well, we can take you to the hospital where your mom works. That way she would know if you had a tetanus shot, and she would have your insurance card. And since she's your mom, she'd have the authority to let you be treated."

April began to feel afraid. "No, I'm not going to a hospital." She pulled away from George very fast and began to stomp out of the garage.

"Hold on there," George said. "Where are you going?"

"Home. I'm going home. My mother will take care of this when she comes home. I'm sorry to have bothered you." And off she went.

April went to the diner and into the bathroom to wash her hands. She had the needle George put down, and she began to fish out the lump of glass on her own. That hurt so much that April started to cry. So she took a big breath, and holding her breath, she tried again. It took a long time because the glass broke into pieces. April slowly worked out every piece and sliver of glass. April felt spent and light-headed. But she took extra precautions, washing her hand with disinfectant soap. She washed her hand over and over.

April came out of the bathroom, and Flo was standing there.

"Are you all right, darling?" she asked.

April held up her hand to show her.

"Oh, Jesus. Jesus. You need medical attention. Now where is the mercurochrome and Band-Aids?" Flo took April to the back room and said, "Now you have to be real brave when I put on the mercurochrome—it burns like fire. I'll blow air on it if it stings too much."

As Flo applied the red medicine with the glass wand, it did sting, but April refused to acknowledge the pain. She stood there like a soldier gritting her teeth, and letting the medicine do its job.

Then Flo applied a large Band-Aid. "Well, aren't you a super trooper. This calls for some ice cream with bananas and whipped cream. What do you say to that?"

April just smiled, and Flo tousled her hair. Soon April was sitting at the kitchen end of the counter stools having her ice cream, and in came the evening crowd. They were teenagers on a Friday night wanting cheeseburgers and fries. Some of the teens were dressed neatly, and some were sloppy, with long baggy pants and long hair. But all of them were noisy, and it got very loud in the diner.

April wasn't half through with her ice cream when in walked the sheriff. He had a lady with him. The teenagers all hollered to the sheriff. Some came up to him, shaking hands or patting him on his arm or his back. Then he spied April.

The sheriff and lady came over to where April was sitting. April looked at the woman who was the prettiest woman she had ever seen—next to her mother, of course. The woman had jet-black hair and dark eyes, and she had the lightest skin she ever saw.

April said, "How do you do?"

The woman answered, "I'm quite well, thank you. Are you enjoying your ice cream?"

"Yes, I am," said April. The conversation began to lag.

So the sheriff motioned for the woman to sit at a table across from where April sat.

"Would you like to sit with us?" he asked April.

"No, thanks," April said. "I'm going to finish this and then go home."

"Oh, that's too bad. I hoped that you would talk to my wife about the fun we had today."

"I will do that another time. It was fun, but I can't stay out much longer." With that, April hopped off the stool, waved goodbye to Flo, and left. She was glad no one had said anything about her hand. She couldn't believe no one saw the big Band-Aid across her palm. It was just as well since it was time to go home and go to sleep. It was had been a stressful day, and April was glad to be heading home.

Things to Do

FLO CAME OVER TO THE sheriff and said, "Gordon, I don't know about that little one. She's as tough as nails," and they laughed.

The sheriff said, "I just wish I knew where she lived. We would love to help the mom out. Miranda could watch her during the day so she wouldn't be roaming the streets while her mother worked."

Flo said, "She doesn't roam too far. She keeps close by and helps just about anyone she comes in contact with. I wish I could keep her here. She washes dishes for me like a trooper, and she never says no to whatever I ask of her. She takes mail to the post office and picks up stamps and supplies. She went with me to the bank, and she's the nicest, most polite little helper."

"I know what you mean," said the sheriff. They all watched April as she made her way across the street past the town hall, heading toward her home.

April came to the house, and the little old man wasn't home. She entered into the basement again, and there waiting for her was Arnold the cat. "Meow," was his greeting. April rubbed his head and stroked his back to his tail. She then went upstairs as fast and as quietly as she could with Arnold following her. April opened the refrigerator, and she was in luck.

The old man must have gone to the grocery store: the refrigerator was full. April took some tangerines, an apple, celery, plums, grapes, and put them in a Ziploc bag. She noticed four jars of peanut butter, and she took one. She also took a sleeve of crackers.

Then April went downstairs to the basement, and took her clothing and washed them in the sink. It sure felt good to be clean. Tomorrow was Saturday, and if the old man went away, then she would do her laundry the right way. And that's what happened. While her laundry was drying, she and Arnold had a nice chicken sandwich with tomato and lettuce, and then some grapes. Arnold appreciated the milk that April couldn't drink. April cleaned up and took her clean clothing with her—not leaving any telltale signs behind.

April went quickly to the field, then the car, and got in. The sky was quiet. There were flashes of light in the sky. Then boom, boom—the lightning and thunder began. Soon the heavy rains came down. April snuggled in the blanket she had, but each time the thunder boomed, she jumped.

April remembered being home on the porch when the summer rains would come. The wind would pick up, and she would snuggle under the blanket beside her momma. The rain would come over the ridge. The wind and rain would go left and right, and it soaked everything. But April felt safe there under that blanket by her momma.

April had to concentrate real hard and hold onto those memories. Momma wasn't here, but she could pretend she was.

April said her prayers and concentrated, and soon she was sound asleep as the wind and rain raged on.

The next morning was like others, and soon April's life had a pattern. That's how April spent her summer in California. Monday mornings were spent at the library, then to George's garage, and ending at the diner. Tuesdays, April put grocery carts into the cart houses. She earned money for the day's supper or for shopping at the Goodwill store. Then she would go home. Since it was senior citizens' day, that gave her the chance to wash and dry her clothing in the old man's basement. She could take a shower or a bath and wash her hair. She was also able to visit and fuss with Arnold the cat.

April wondered when the old man was going to take all the boxes with that name on them away, but they were always there each time she went into the basement. On those days, April also had fresh fruit and vegetables from the unknown generosity of the old man. There was always a home-cooked meal in the refrigerator, and April helped herself until she was full, which wasn't much at all. On Wednesdays, April went to town to the Goodwill to shop. She could spend hours there looking at books and trying on shoes or clothing. April would then walk to the garage and see George and Katie. April always got a kick out of taking calls and putting the work in the appointment book. George loved her taking that responsibility. He was usually busy, and April did a good job. She was smart and a great hostess—making coffee for his customers and turning on the radio in the afternoon to hear the news.

April usually ended her Wednesdays at the diner for Flo's famous, delicious chili and corn bread. After dinner, she walked home to the old car. The crazy dog that scared her, never came anymore. April thought he'd either run away, or they may have moved.

On Thursdays, April went to the town market store. It was her favorite place. It was a place for fresh fruit and vegetables, lunch meat, and any tool you could ever need. She discovered the hardware store had much more than tools. In the very back of the store, they always had a barrel with a checkerboard game in progress.

There were also horse harnesses on the walls for sale, horse blankets, bridles, halters and all types of livestock needs: pitchforks, shovels, rope, saddles, cow kickers, coveralls, lined jeans, and so much more. April loved to go there and smell the fresh leather.

The owner of the store's name was George Rex, he and his lovely wife worked there together. Evelyn operated the post office and took care of customers. George loved when April came to the store. He was always excited to see her.

He would give her a sandwich with fresh-cut meat on homemade bread slathered with mustard, just the way April liked it, with a side dish of cottage cheese. Often, he would sit there at the barrels and teach her how to play checkers, game after game, and in time, April became a stealthy player. He would put her to work in the back of the store washing meat trays. She helped him clean the meat counter, especially inside where he couldn't reach. He always gave April a nice hunk of lunch meat to take home to her momma. April always thanked him. He would use his hand in a downward motion as if to say, "Aw, it's all right."

April loved both of them. They were so kind, they reminded her of her grandparents. April did have a grandpa she loved dearly. She wondered if they thought about her. She wished they could meet Evelyn and George and see how kind and thrifty they were. It was always a surprise to see what Evelyn had for April as she would get ready to leave the store.

"Oh, where are you going?" she would say to April. "You come over here." Then she would bring out a bag with either a pair of blue jeans, a shirt, or a sweet treat for her to take home. Everyone, everyone in town, believed April when she said that her momma was a nurse and worked a lot of overtime. It was a big fat lie that she had to keep for her safety. That's how April saw it. So many good, kind, genuine people that trusted and believed her made April feel so guilty. But it had to be that way for now.

Often April went exploring, watching the crop workers, or sometimes shopping at the Goodwill store. April loved to look at books. Sometimes she curled up in a corner and, looked at pictures for hours. Sometimes you could figure out the story by the pictures. April liked to look at the clothing, although she didn't need much. Barbara had bought her underclothing and socks, and she had shorts and shirts, but nevertheless April enjoyed looking. April dearly loved books, and they weren't very expensive at the Goodwill store. Sometimes a dime would buy a big book, but April knew that it was near impossible to read in that car, because it had no lights. Even in the basement of the old man's home, she dared not turn on any lights to read. No matter what, April always found a book with great pictures that intrigued her. There were also poems with pictures and history books with photos of swords. She also loved to look at encyclopedia. April always took a book along with her, whether she could read it or not.

Back Home

BACK HOME, THERE WAS A picture of April hanging in the post office, also one in the county courthouse. Sometimes her picture was featured in the local newspaper under Lost. The state police kept looking for her, hoping to get a lead on a found child. But in the past six months, there had been nothing—not one shred of evidence, not one report.

Momma had a hope that April was alive, and she clung to that in her prayers. It was the only way she could keep her sanity. Many family members expressed sympathy as if April were dead. But in her heart, Momma knew, she just knew, her daughter was alive.

The grandfather also felt that this wasn't the end. For an unknown reason, he too felt his granddaughter was alive. He knew her very well, and she had a strong spirit within her. April was an adventurous, smart, kind, loving girl. He couldn't imagine anything bad happening to her. Someone had to have her and appreciate the goodness in this child.

Otherwise, no one missed her outwardly. If they did, they didn't mention a word about her in public or with their own family. The two brothers wondered, but they said nothing out of fear. They had a deep secret to keep. Only in their prayers at bedtime was their sister mentioned, in such a way of hope to keep her safe and keep them safe as well.

The days passed into weeks, and then weeks into months, season after season, holiday after holiday without her. It sometimes took the breath away from Momma, but she endured. She had faith and believed.

The Truth

Back in Fresno, it was a sunny Saturday morning. April combed her hair and pinned back her bangs with bobby pins. She headed toward the diner. It was breakfast time, and she had earned four dollars the day before. She wanted to eat a good breakfast today, because tomorrow was Sunday. She didn't eat out or buy anything on a Sunday.

April made sure every one of her possessions was in place. She closed the car door and walked down the street. As she walked, she noticed the migrant workers were gone. The harvest was over, and soon school would be starting. April missed seeing the farmers and had hoped to meet the children she had seen so often. She wondered how old the little girl she had seen earlier was. She had hoped they could have become friends. April's hand had healed nicely. There was no scar.

At the diner, there was a crowd, so April slipped to the back of the counter to an end stool. She waited for Flo or another waitress patiently taking her turn.

"Hey, kiddo. What will you have today?" Flo greeted her cheerfully. "I would like some pancakes please and a glass of milk." To April, this wasn't just a diner. Flo was sort of like a mother to her. She fed her and gave her more than she asked for. But April never asked for much.

Flo loved to cook as did April's mother, so in that sense, both mothers were alike.

After breakfast, April scooted around the customers seated at the counter to pay for her meal. The waitress took her slip and said, "Paid for." April didn't understand. The waitress pointed over to a table, and as April looked, she saw it was the sheriff. He was there for breakfast too with some of his deputies.

The sheriff nodded at her and waved. April waved back, mouthing, "Thank you," to him. Then out the door she went, skipping along. Then she realized she'd forgotten to bring her notebook along to the garage.

Last week, she'd found an interesting article at the library about new mechanical tools. She had put that page into the notebook of her suitcase to give to George. April felt she should go and get it before she went to the garage. As she walked along, she heard a loud engine sound, like a bulldozer. She decided to take the long walk around by the park. She sat on a swing for a while and then saw a nest of red ants. She made sure to leave them alone.

April came to the top of the street where she stayed, and as she walked along, she felt that something looked very different. She wasn't positive what it was until she came to the old man's little house. There was a huge swath of grass that had been ripped or dragged away. As she walked farther, panic hit her. The car, her home, was gone! April was so shocked the car was gone. Some of the tree branches had broken off. Also, there was a big path that the car must have made as it was pulled over the top, scraping the grass away.

April began to cry. She didn't know where to go, and she thought of Flo. As she walked along, April felt as if she couldn't breathe. She couldn't think anymore. She was frightened and confused. She felt numb.

At the diner, she turned the knob but never heard the bell. She went inside, and she didn't hear anyone. The silence in her ears was deafening.

Flo saw her and came out from behind the counter.

She bent down in front of April and asked, "What's the matter, sweetheart?"

April couldn't answer her. She just sobbed with deep breaths. Flo took April to the back of the diner and held her close to her.

"Come on, April. I can't help you unless you tell me what's wrong," Flo gently told her.

April looked at Flo with her eyes full of tears, and said, "I'm a wiar, a cwiminal. I'll go to jail," and she kept crying uncontrollably.

Flo motioned for a waitress to come to her. Flo held April close to her so April wouldn't hear. Flo told the waitress to call the sheriff right away. Flo was concerned someone had hurt April or had her do something April knew not to.

Sheriff Gordon Di Angelo got the call via radio in his cruiser to come to the diner right away. He had just left the diner minutes ago and couldn't imagine what tragic event had happened in that small space of time. The sheriff turned the cruiser around at the end of the street, and he got there as fast as he could.

He wondered to himself what could have happened. Was it a robbery? No, it couldn't have been that, or the dispatch would have said so. He drove as fast as he could and screeched to a halt right in front of the diner. He left the cruiser running and went in the diner to see what the emergency was.

As he came inside the diner, there was no commotion. It was the usual customers enjoying meals, until he looked to the back and saw a very frightened April crying. Flo was sitting holding April, wiping her tears away, saying over and over, "It's going to be all right, honey."

The sheriff strode up to the table, pulled out a chair, and sat down across from April. Seeing the torment in this little girl was twisting his heart into knots. "Is there something I can do?" he asked April, tapping her lightly on her arm.

April looked at him. She couldn't see clearly because of the tears in her eyes. She placed her arms over the top of the table and said in a babbling blur, "Awest me. I'm a cwiminal. I have wied to eweryone, and I should go to jail." April cried harder, tears running down her cheeks and dripping off her nose.

The sheriff almost laughed, but he felt such sympathy for this little girl. "What have you done so terrible that you should go to jail?" he asked her.

She looked up so pitifully, looked directly into his eyes, and said, "I have stole things, I have wied over and over to be safe, and now I have wost evewything. Evewything that I had is all gone," she breathlessly said. Her words weren't clear, she was so upset!

"Let's start with this. What have you lost?" he asked her.

She told him about living in the car. "I wost myr tiger, and my cwothing, the suitcase wif my family's pikturs, my backpok thing, and my notiebook and all my (sniff) books, and ewerything." It all came spilling out.

The sheriff was shocked when he realized this little girl had been living on her own for over six months. There was no momma! So he did the best thing he knew to do. He got up and, using the diner's telephone, he called his wife. "Miranda, I don't know what you're doing, but, dear, drop it right now. Come down to the diner as fast as you can, and as calmly as you can. I need your help," and he hung up the phone.

Within fifteen minutes, Miranda Di Angelo came in the diner

door. She saw her husband and then that small little girl who was crumbled in grief. Miranda came to her. "Hello, April. You know me. I'm Miranda, the sheriff's wife. I would like very much if you could come with me, so I can help you. All right?"

April had no fight in her. She was defeated. She viewed herself as a criminal and went willingly. But she asked, "Do I need handcuffs to go with you?"

"No, darling, you don't," Miranda said, hoisting April up on her hip, walking out, and placing her in her car.

Meanwhile, the sheriff had an idea about which car April had been talking about. He drove his car to the spot, and he too saw what had happened. He got out of his squad car and knocked on the old man's door.

The old man came to the door, opening it to the sheriff with a smile.

"Hello, Jonas. How are you?" the sheriff said. "I see your old Ford is gone. Did you sell it for restoration or for salvage?"

The old man told him it was for scrap, and that it went to Buzzard's Junkyard on the other side of town.

The sheriff stood there and said, "You know, Jonas, I've meant to stop time after time since Elaine passed away, but time and my job always got in the way. It was a lovely service. I spoke to you that day, but I want to apologize to you. I'm regrettably sorry."

Then Jonas held out his hand, and the two men shook hands. The sheriff thanked him, got back into his squad car, and headed to the other side of town to Buzzard's Junkyard.

Once there, Gordon got out and was greeted by the manager of the scrapyard, who was also the owner.

"Hello, Homer," the sheriff said. "By chance, did you get in an old Ford for scrap today?"

"As a matter of fact, we did," Homer answered.

"Have you put it into a block yet, or is it still intact?" the sheriff asked.

"Oh, it's all together yet. It's right over there along the side yard. Why? Are you interested in salvaging it for yourself?" asked Homer.

"Oh no. Just a part of an investigation," the sheriff answered as they walked toward the old Ford.

When they got to the car, the sheriff noticed right away the things April mentioned. "May I have these things?" Gordon asked Homer.

"Oh, sure you can. Here let me help you." And soon the suitcase, clothing, notebooks, books, and tiger were all in the back of the sheriff's car. The two men had a brief exchange of conversation, and the sheriff headed back to town. He reached for the phone in his car and called the diner.

"Hello, Flo's diner," said Flo on the other end.

"Flo, can you tell me if Miranda and April are still at the diner?"

"Oh, no. They left here ten minutes ago," answered Flo.

"Okay then, thank you," said the sheriff. He decided that, since it was only one o'clock, it would be good sense to go home to his wife and see what happened. He could return to work after that.

At home, Miranda decided it would be good for April to have a bath. April was resigned to do anything, and perhaps a nice warm bath would make her feel better. Miranda got out one of her husband's

T-shirts for April to wear. After the bath, Miranda worked the tangles out of April's curly hair.

They then went downstairs. Miranda lifted April onto her lap and rocked her. April buried her head in Miranda's chest with tears and big sighs. There was little to console her. Miranda tried constant rocking as she stroked April's hair and back. What a horrible thing to have a child living in the streets. Who in the world would do such a thing to her? Now there was another family member equally upset and concerned about April. That was the very spoiled and loved Ruby, their terrier.

Before long, Miranda's husband came home, and he was carrying a load of all sorts of odd things with him. He came into the living room beside the rocking chair and said in a whisper to April, "Hey, you. Lookie here at what I have," and April looked.

Her eyes flew wide open, she became alive, as if she'd seen her best friend. Ruby was happy too. She barked and stood on her back legs to celebrate with April.

"My things! How ever did you find them?" she asked as she fondled them like treasures. The tears stopped, and she was elated and calm.

"Now, do you think you can help me understand what happened to you? Can you do that for me?" Gordon asked April.

"Yes, I can," she said. And April told the sheriff the entire story of how her home life had been, how two of her brothers took many lickings for her, and promised her a better life. April told them how her brothers said for her to be brave and kind, and to have fun. April told them about the bus trip to Carruthers, the many people she had met on the bus, and on vacation with Barbara. She told him everything. She wasn't sure where she started. She just knew it was home.

The sheriff was stunned and also impressed that this little girl had not only lived but thrived living on her own. She was a resourceful, reserved, and intelligent little girl. He knew many adults who wouldn't have done as well under the same circumstances.

"Well, how about you stay here with my wife and me?" the sheriff said.

April looked directly at him and said, "You mean I don't have to go to jail?" She was quiet serious.

He couldn't help but smile. "No, no nothing of that sort. You stay here with my wife. I'll be home before you know it, and visit with you. I'm sure the two of you will find something to do."

With that, he kissed his wife, hugged her, and headed out the door.

April looked at Miranda and asked, "Does he always kiss you like that when he goes away?"

"Always!" was Miranda's reply.

The two of them read a book together, and then the woman said, "I need to make dinner for Gordon. Would you like to help?"

"Me? Okay," said April. "What are you going to make?"

"I thought I would make spaghetti and meatballs. Do you like that?" she asked April.

"Oh, yes, I do, but I don't think I should eat his food," replied April.

The woman said, "April, this is not just Gordon's food. It's for all of us."

April watched as Mrs. Di Angelo went about getting dinner ready. April soon wandered into the living room and sat on the couch with her tiger. She sat there looking at the tiger, realizing he had made the long trip with her, and she hugged him close to her. Very soon, she began to snuggle on the couch and was asleep. Her new faithful companion Ruby stayed at her side and wouldn't leave April.

Mrs. Di Angelo came in and saw her sleeping. She carefully picked her up and carried her upstairs to a bedroom she had long ago made for a little girl she had hoped for but wasn't blessed to have. They had tried so often over the years, but she couldn't carry a child more than three months. It was too much, too painful. She and her husband both decided it wasn't meant to be. And here right before her lay a perfectly beautiful little girl who had no home, no mother, no one to care for her. And the maternal instincts of Miranda Di Angelo began to grow. If it were up to her, and if God was willing, this little one would be theirs. She knelt down right then and offered a prayer. She asked God in his mercy to grant, if it wasn't too much to ask, that this little one, who had no one, be for her and her dear, sweet husband.

All that while, Ruby too seemed to be praying, her paws were crossed. And there was no way she would leave April, not ever.

They had tried to have a child so many times only to be left disappointed, always left full of sorrow. But now, this just happened. April came into their lives, and she had no one. "Please God, if it be thy will, we are willing to do whatever we can to have her stay and live with us, and be our child."

Miranda went back downstairs to compose herself. Very soon, her husband, Sheriff Gordon Di Angelo, came in the door. "How are you, sweetheart?" he said, kissing her on her cheek.

She smiled and said, "I'm fine. Your dinner is just about ready."

"Where is she?" he asked.

"*She* is upstairs, fast asleep," said Miranda.

"No. You're kidding me," he said.

"No, I'm not. She had a bath and was worn out," Miranda said. "Careful! Ruby is with her and has decided April is hers."

Gordon came to his wife and put his arms around her waist. He whispered in her ear, "Maybe our wishes have come true."

"Don't say that," she said. "I'm hopeful, but afraid."

"Who? Who would let such a beautiful, healthy young one like her go away on her own? There has to be someone looking for her."

Gordon sat at the table as his wife placed a plate of spaghetti topped with meatballs and sauce in front of him.

"Aren't you eating with me, sweetie?" he asked.

She said, "A little. I'll have just a little. I don't want my nerves to wrestle with my stomach."

Gordon sat looking at his wife and said, "I'm going to call Du Val tomorrow. He'll know what would be best for all of us. Meanwhile, we'll enjoy her for as long as we can."

Miranda looked soulfully at her husband.

"I know," she said. "I know. It's not that. I know she's not ours, but I can't help but feel this is right. She's a gift. Have you ever in your life heard of something like this happening to anyone, ever?"

"No, I haven't," Gordon said. "Sadly, when I get a call about a child, it's usually bad news. The child is done away with. But we're going to do this right, for her and for us. I know that Du Val will know what to do—the right course." He got up and placed both of their dishes in the sink.

"I'll get those," his wife said.

Gordon went upstairs to take a shower, but he couldn't resist peeking in at the little girl in the child's room they'd prepared twelve years ago. April was lying on her right side, facing him. She looked so peaceful, so small. And he too felt the strong emotions of a father. He tried to push those feelings away, but he couldn't. He wouldn't.

Dang it! Standing there he promised to never let anyone, or anything hurt her so long as he lived. He knew his wife's feelings, and his mirrored hers. They were good people. He supported his wife, and they could easily afford a child of their own. They were well respected in the community. They'd tried to have children of their own, but for whatever reason it didn't happen. Maybe God felt that perhaps they didn't deserve a child or didn't have his blessing. Gordon didn't want to believe that, but the disappointment over the last twelve years had been difficult. He would never allow Miranda to blame herself, but Gordon felt he was to blame. Maybe he worked too hard at his job, maybe, maybe, but there were no answers. They had both been to clinics. They were healthy adults, but each time the fetus didn't survive. Twelve years of disappointment, and for some reason, this little one had caught his eye six months ago.

Now here she was, lying in this room, under his roof. Emotions spilled over, and he felt tears well into his eyes. Gordon Di Angelo wasn't a man of tears. It was a rare thing for him. He showered and went downstairs.

His wife was sitting in her recliner watching TV. Gordon sat on the couch near her, and asked for the newspaper. She handed the paper to him as if striking him, and he replied, saying, "Oh, yeah. You think so?"

He got up and began to smother his wife in kisses, tickling her.

"Gordon, stop," she said, laughing. But he didn't stop, and soon they both headed upstairs to their own room.

Ruby was snuggled in beside April. Gordon called her, but Ruby wasn't going to budge. As sternly as he could in a whisper he said, "Ruby, come." Ruby rolled over behind April and snuggled deeper into the covers. Miranda pulled her husband's arm to go to bed. There was nothing they could do—once Ruby made up her mind, that was it. She was, after all, a terrier.

April awoke early. She found the bathroom with the help of a night-light that was in the bathroom. She headed downstairs and sat there in the dark. Soon Gordon came down. He was casually doing his routine. He would come downstairs in his underwear and dress in the kitchen. He almost jumped out of his skin when he saw April sitting there in the dark.

Immediately, he tried to cover up with a pillow that was nearby. April giggled at the sight of him.

"What's so funny?" he asked her.

"You! You don't need to cover up. It's just like a bathing suit." Gordon could see her reasoning, but he felt that would be the last time he came down the stairs like that. From now on, he would dress in his bedroom and come downstairs fully dressed in his work clothes.

Gordon hurried into the kitchen to put on his barn clothing that were in the cedar closet in the kitchen. He put on his regular jeans and shirt, then grabbed his boots. As he was pulling them on, April came out and asked, "Where are you going?" Ruby was right beside her.

"I have animals to take care of before I go to work. You can wait in here, or you can come along with me."

"I'm coming," she said. And she went out just as she was—in her underwear, his T-shirt, no shoes, nothing else. April slipped her hand into his as they walked in the dark to the barn.

At the barn, Gordon switched the lights on, and there in the barn were five ponies. April almost lost her breath. She walked over to a brown pony with a black mane and tail.

"I used to have a pony just like this one," she said. "Does she have a name?"

Gordon looked at the tag on the stall door. "Dobbins, her name is Dobbins."

Gordon picked up a manure fork, grabbed the wheelbarrow, and began picking stalls clean. He gave fresh water and hay to each of them. April was soon at his elbow, filling buckets when he wasn't, and picking stalls whenever he let go of the manure fork. Gordon couldn't help but be amused at how comical she looked in that T-shirt trying to lift the manure into the wheelbarrow. He had to give her credit. She wasn't lazy. She wanted to work and knew her way around as if she had done this type of work before. In twenty minutes, they were done.

"You're quite a good helper," he told her.

"I know," said April.

"Well, we better go back in and have some breakfast. Then I need to change to go to work."

In they went, and the noises from the kitchen soon brought Miranda Di Angelo downstairs to see.

"Who made those dirty footprints in my kitchen?" she said.

April looked down at the floor and realized those footprints were hers.

"I did it," she said.

"Yes. I know it was you," Miranda said, tousling April's hair.

"Are you going to be home at noon for lunch, Mr. Di Angelo?" she asked.

"Oh. Yes, ma'am. I wouldn't miss it for the world," and he pulled her close to him and kissed her lips.

April put her hands over her eyes.

"April, do you like cereal, or do you want toast?"

"I would rather have toast. If you don't mind?" April answered. And the three of them sat having breakfast. Ruby was begging when Miranda told her to get her own food in her dish.

Gordon couldn't help but reflect how nice this was, like a dream come true. Then casually he looked at his watch and said, "I have got to get moving." He went upstairs to get dressed. Miranda followed him after telling April she would just be a few minutes.

Upstairs, Gordon told Miranda about what innocently happened that morning. Then he asked her to have his clothing upstairs in another bedroom so he could dress before he went downstairs. He wanted both of them to be aware there was an innocent one living there, not just the two of them anymore. Miranda agreed, and hugged her husband.

"I love you, sweetheart. You have a wonderful morning. I think I'm going to take her to get some new underclothing at the five-and-dime today. If that's all right?"

"Sure, it is. Maybe I'll see you in town," he said. With that he kissed his wife goodbye, and headed to work.

April was still sitting at the table. "Are you still eating?" he asked her as he put on his work shoes. They were shiny and black.

"No, not really," she replied. Gordon saw a piece of toast sitting on April's plate, and he reached for it. April put her hand on it before he could. She lifted it up for Gordon to take a bite. He did, and then he bent over to kiss April's cheek. Then he was out the door and gone.

April sat there. She touched the cheek he had kissed and wondered why he'd done that. It sure was nice, and she missed having affection shown to her. She slid off of the chair, and put her plate in the sink. Soon Miranda was at her side.

Miranda bent down eye to eye with April and said, "Would you like to go to town today, and we can buy you some new underclothing?"

April just stood there looking at her. She put her arms around Miranda's neck and said, "May I just stay here with you?" Miranda was suddenly emotional. She was touched deeply. This wasn't expected.

"Oh, sure we can. But I would like to buy you some new undie things. Yours are wearing through. See?" And she tugged on the waistband of April's underwear.

It was true she did need newer things. She had outgrown much of the clothing she had brought with her. She couldn't wash her clothing regularly the way other children had theirs washed while she was living in the car.

After the breakfast dishes were in the dishwasher and the beds were made, Miranda laid out clothing for April to wear.

The weather was still warm, in the high seventies, so shorts were all right. April got dressed, and the two of them walked to the garage at the far end of the house. Miranda opened the small door to the garage. Then she opened the car's passenger back seat door for April. Miranda told her it was safer for her to sit in the back seat.

April climbed in, and Miranda put a seatbelt across her belly and chest, clicking the belt into place. Miranda got in and started the sedan. She pressed a button, and the garage doors began to go up on their own. Then Miranda buckled in too.

April was surprised and laughed at the doors. "It's not magic, April. This is a garage door opener. I can open and close the garage doors with this." She pulled her sedan out slowly, then she closed the doors. April had to watch the doors until they were completely down.

"That's neat," April said. Miranda smiled and told April it's an electric door opener, not a toy. On to town they went. In no time at all they were downtown, and Miranda parked the sedan. She helped April out, and they went shopping.

Gordon Di Angelo, however, was on a mission. As soon as he got to work, he looked over the plans for the day to see who was on the schedule to work. He looked to see if there were any court hearings that he had to be at, and there were none. He sat down and dialed his friend since grade school, Judge Newell Du Val.

The phone rang once, twice, and a woman answered, "Hello, Judge Du Val's office. How may I help you?"

"Hey. Hello there, Missy. Is Newell in? This is Sheriff Di Angelo."

Missy said, "He is. Can you wait a minute?"

"Sure. Sure, I can," he answered her. Missy was the judge's niece. She was planning on going to college to study criminal law, but she wanted to work a year or two to save up money.

"Hello, you old turd," the judge said, answering the phone.

Gordon laughed. "Is that any way to greet an old friend?" Both of the men laughed over the phone.

"Listen, I have a situation come up of a sensitive nature. I need to sit and talk with you in private—the sooner, the better. I need professional advice," Gordon said.

"Well, I gave you professional advice when I told you Miranda and I would have made a better couple than the two of you," the judge said, and they both laughed again.

"No. This is serious. We like to joke around, but might you have a small space of time, say, fifteen minutes?" Gordon asked.

"Well, I'll tell you what. How about we have lunch? I'll break down and spend two crummy dollars on your worthless hide," the judge answered.

"Well, that's mighty generous of you, but I already have lunch plans with two beautiful ladies," Gordon said.

"I see," said the judge. "For you to walk away from a free lunch, this must be serious. Come by today around ten o'clock. We have some open time then, but I must be in court by eleven," said Judge Du Val.

Gordon was relieved, "Thanks! I'll see you at ten in your office." They both said goodbye and hung up.

The telephone never rang, the paperwork was all in order, and the minutes ticked by so very slowly. It was the eighth time Sheriff

Di Angelo looked at the big clock on the wall. It was only nine ten, so Sheriff Di Angelo picked up the wanted files and reviewed them. It listed bank robbers in Freeport that may be heading this way, and a lost dog, hm. There was nothing else.

Soon one of the deputies came in.

"Hey, Bobby. What's going on?" the sheriff asked the deputy.

"Nothing much. If you have something to do, I can cover for you. No reports on the CB, nothing" he said.

"Well, I do have a 10:00 o'clock appointment at the judge's chambers today," Gordon said.

"Is it about the runaways?" Bobby asked, and Gordon's blood froze in his veins for a minute. Then he recalled that three weeks ago there were three young runaway girls, teenagers who decided to go to Los Angeles to find jobs, and hoped to become famous.

"Oh, no. Not that. It's something else entirely," Gordon said, relieved. Gordon got busy refiling reports. He hated when papers were in the wrong file. If someone appealed their conviction, there could be a retrial. If you just grabbed a person's file, you had better look inside the file. Often deputies were careless and filed papers in the wrong folders, which would be very embarrassing.

In no time, it was five of 10:00 a.m. Gordon grabbed his hat, and headed out the door. It was a five-minute drive to the courthouse and the judge's chambers. As he drove, Gordon reflected on all the many years he and Newell had been friends. Since grade school, he guessed. They had been in Cub Scouts, gone to elementary school together, then middle school, and Boy Scouts. They'd played on the same football team in high school. They'd both loved their little town, and both vowed to never leave it. There had been much to do to improve the town and make it better back then. Yes, they had big plans as teenagers.

The judge in particular was born serious, but to Gordon, he was as light-hearted and open as when they were kids. That was a good thing. Everyone needs time to just be themselves, not be judged—no pun intended.

Gordon parked his truck, since he didn't think it was right to use the squad car for personal business. He walked up the front steps to the front door. There was a scanner there. You had to place your keys in a basket and remove items from your pockets: any lose money or change, anything metal, as it would set off the metal detector.

Instinctively, Gordon removed his pistol from the holster, placing it into the basket as well. One of the men at the scanner was new and raised his eyebrows in concern when he saw the pistol.

The other man, Jake, had been on this job from the beginning. He pushed the new man aside and said, "Give our sheriff some respect. Will ya?"

The new man backed away and put out his hand as if in apology.

"It's all right, Jake. He's just doing his job," said Gordon.

"Well, he had better learn who is who." Jake said. Gordon replied, "It's is a good thing. You never know who you can trust these days, so it didn't hurt for him to question me. Now he knows. But always check—you never know."

Then Gordon picked up his revolver and keys and headed to the judge's chambers. Gordon knocked on the door, and he heard his friend say, "Come on in, you scoundrel." Gordon stepped in, and there was his friend, the judge, feet propped up on his desk, reclining back in his chair.

"I see our tax dollars are working very hard," Gordon jabbed back at his friend.

Newell stood up, and shook Gordon's hand. "How are ya? What's this serious problem you have?"

Gordon sat down, and said, "Have you noticed a little girl walking around Carruthers the last few months?"

"No, I don't go out looking for little girls," Newell said.

"Come on, I'm being serious," Gordon said.

"Yes, I see that," Newell replied. "Okay, let's hear it from the beginning."

Gordon began. He told how April had been put on a bus by her two young brothers, whose only intent was to save her from their abusive father. Gordon didn't know which state in the East April had boarded that bus. He thought maybe Delaware or New Jersey. April didn't know either.

It was six months, maybe seven in all, that April had been gone. This included the time she stayed with a very kind woman who'd left a note in April's backpack and up to the time she arrived here. And she'd lived in Carruthers for the last six months.

Gordon told Newell he searched for "the aunt," but no one had reported her missing—not in any UPI wire and no Amber alerts. Gordon casually said to Newell of how much he and Miranda wanted a child of their own. Of any of his friends or acquaintances, Newell was the one who knew and understood Gordon better than anyone. Judge Newell Du Val had the privilege of spending time with his friend at each miscarriage, and there had been many.

"Can you help us?" Gordon asked, "Do you know what to do in a case like this?"

Newell looked at his friend. "Yes, of course. We'll begin an adoption process, and we must put out a search for her parents. If she has any. You don't know my friend. There are those parents who sell children for money, or it might be she was stolen and got away. In any case, we'll begin the process, and if no one comes forward in two years from the time we file, then she can be yours. So let me have Missy draw up the paperwork, and we'll get things started on this end. I suggest you send out a request for missing persons in the eastern states. We have to be sure.

"I'll have Missy call you later on in the week for you and Miranda to come in, and bring the girl with you. I would like to spend some time alone with her. Sometimes children tell the least likely person more of the truth," Newell said.

Gordon stood up and thanked his friend. They shook hands and Newell said, "Don't worry. If it's meant to be, it will be."

Gordon agreed. He turned to leave, closing the door behind him. Gordon felt as if a large weight had been lifted off of his shoulders. Gordon knew it was best to be honest in this situation, for all of their sakes. It would be awful if they adopted April, and then a parent would come out of somewhere with court hearings and so on. So he felt at ease with the route they were going to take.

Outside, Gordon stood on the steps of the courthouse for a minute, and then went to his truck and headed home for lunch with "his girls."

Gordon pulled into the driveway and noticed his wife's car. He went inside to the kitchen. There was a large pizza box on the table, and the two ladies were in the living room with the television on. They were singing and dancing to a song with Mr. Rogers. Ruby was right in the mix, barking and more alive than she had been in a year. What a beautiful sight!

They didn't notice Gordon until he said, "Hello, anyone home?" His wife came into the kitchen, and kissed him, followed by April who hugged his legs. He felt like he was ten feet tall. *So this is what it's like to be a daddy*, he thought.

They sat down together and had pizza. Half of the pizza was cheese, the other half cheese and pepperoni. Ruby was content to have a piece of crust that April had sneaked to her under the table.

"Which do you want?" he asked April.

"I would like plain cheese, please," she answered. They talked, laughed, ate, and talked some more. He heard all about their shopping experience. Gordon saw how happy his wife was. Her eyes said everything.

All too soon, lunchtime was over, and Gordon had to leave to go back to the police station. He reached for his wife and kissed her. Then he gave April a kiss on her forehead.

"I'll see you two beautiful girls tonight," he said smiling, and then he was gone.

The next morning Gordon came down the stairs dressed in his work jeans. Gordon saw April asleep on the couch and wondered if she'd had a nightmare since she wasn't up in bed. He went outside quietly to do the usual chores, and to his surprise they were all done. He was astounded. Each stall was picked clean, and all of the horses and ponies had hay and fresh water. The chickens were fed, and the eggs were all gone.

Gordon went back into the house, and then he saw April's little sneakers had sawdust on them, and the egg basket was on the counter. What a little stinker and sweetheart she was! Gordon couldn't contain himself. He went to April, scooping her up in his arms, and kissed her cheeks. As she awoke, she was laughing.

"When did you go outside and do all the chores?" he asked her.

"Oh, I don't sleep late. I like to get up early and do things. That's all," April said.

Soon Miranda was down, and she too was surprised that April had gone out on her own to do the chores. "Aren't you afraid of the horses? They are so big," she asked her.

"No, I'm not afraid of them. I love them, and they love me. I know it. I see it in their eyes," was her reply.

Each day went like this, all week long. April showed no fear whatsoever around any of the animals. She blazed through any needed job.

It seemed as if the animals called to her. They nickered and pawed for her attention. They all wanted her to tend to them. All of them were impatient, wanting for her to come to them first. April had her own routine, and Gordon was impressed.

The week flew by. On Friday afternoon at 1:00 p.m., Gordon, Miranda, and April sat in the hallway, waiting to see Judge Du Val. The judge had been delayed in a court hearing. They had to wait until the hearing was over. Soon the judge came out, walking down the hallway with his robe flowing around him, slightly touching the floor. April thought it looked silly for a man to be wearing a dress.

Judge Newell Du Val greeted his friends, and invited them to follow him. As they entered his chambers, the judge looked at April and asked her, "May I talk with you alone, just me and you?"

April looked at Gordon and Miranda, and they said, "It's okay, go." She took the judge's hand and followed him. They went into a room full of books. The judge noticed April looking at them.

"Do you like books?" he asked her.

"Oh, yes I do. I love to read," she said. "But I'm not so good at reading big words yet," she said.

The judge laughed, "I'm not an expert either. So how old are you April?" he asked her.

"I'm six going on seven, I believe. I think I might be seven now," she said.

"Do you know when your birthday is—the month and day?" he asked her.

"I was born in April, on the thirteenth, but I don't know what year."

The judge scribbled on a paper. "Do you know your mother's name or your father's name, the parents you left behind? Maybe you know their real first name and last name?" he asked her.

"No, I don't know," she said with her head bent down. Then looking up, she said, "I know I had a lot of brothers. Some didn't like me, and they were mean to me because Poppa told them to treat me mean. I heard Poppa say so. But there were two brothers who were very kind and good to me."

"Can you tell me their names?" the judge asked.

"Tim and John," she replied.

"How old are Tim and John?" the judge asked her.

"I'm not sure," she said.

"Do you remember the state you lived in with your family?" he asked.

"No, I don't know the name of the state, but we lived on a farm, a dairy farm. My momma did the milking with big machines. I would walk to the barn, and Momma would put me in the calf pen with the baby calves. They were all so cute," April remembered.

"I know many things about what was there, but not the name of the city. I was just starting to learn our telephone number, it was something like 2468, or 2248 maybe. That's all I know." April was disappointed in herself.

"When you said some were mean to you, can you tell me what they did to you?" the judge asked her.

April looked at him and began to tell a long, very long story of sadness, abuse, neglect, bruises, and stitches. She showed him the many scars. April didn't tell him *all* the hateful stories, but more than enough. She was quite matter of fact about all of it, as though what had happened to her was routine, a normal life.

That disturbed the judge greatly. "Okay," the judge said. "Come over here," and he lifted her up, and put her sitting on his desk in front of him. "Will you tell me the truth, the whole truth, and swear it to God?"

Solemnly, April bowed her head to think, "What I told you is true, but I don't want to swear to God. You see, I have lied a lot to many people here in this town, not to be mean, but to protect myself. I had to keep this secret. Do you understand? And I'm ashamed of myself. I'm hoping God forgives me all the things that I did, like stealing food and lying. Those are sins, and I did them."

April's eyes were welling up with tears. Judge Newell Du Val was quite moved. His heart was pierced seeing this innocent little girl in torment over such small infractions. She never hurt anyone, and he felt the depth of her pain in his heart. How many times he'd had adults confess, and rarely did they have the pure intent that she did. They wouldn't reveal their true selves.

Perhaps it was innocence, but who's to say an adult can't be innocent, so long as they profess their sins, repent, and ask the Savior for forgiveness? God's love is infinite. His Grace is sufficient. It can be overwhelming. They don't want to admit anything. They cover up with trust issues, but the terms are about themselves. Are they loved? Are they worthy? Can they be worthy?

But to simplify, they must believe in Jesus Christ, get on their knees, and tell God. Pour out your heart and give, and he will give ten times more. The scriptures read, "Ask and ye shall receive." Even if you don't believe. Pray and pour out your heart, and you'll know soon enough.

The judge felt as if he had been punched in the stomach by a very strong man. It was almost revolting to hear of how this little girl "lived," if you can call it that. There had been no structure. She'd had to protect herself on her own from abuse. April had made it crystal clear that her mother loved her. She'd also loved her two brothers and grandfather, and she missed them dearly.

Then the judge said, "Let's change the subject, April. Do you like the Di Angelos, both Gordon and Miranda?"

April's eyes lit up, "Yes. Oh, yes, I do," she said.

"Tell me why," the judge asked her.

April thought for a minute and said, "Because they are nice to me. I always wanted to be treated nice, to not get hit, or get whippings with a belt or switch. To be able to talk when I wanted to, and not be afraid to sleep or go places in my own house. I feel safe with them. I feel like they want me there. You see my momma couldn't stop my poppa. I was afraid to live there."

The two of them sat there, looking at the each other.

The judge asked her, "April, may I ask you a favor?"

April waited a few seconds, and then said, "Yes."

"Will you be my friend? Will you come to me when you have a

problem, if you're afraid, or if there's any time you want to talk with me about anything. May I ask that of you?" the judge said.

"Sure," April said. "I like you, and I think you're very nice."

And with that, he leaned forward and kissed April's forehead. He stood up, set her on the floor, and returned to his chambers where the Di Angelos were waiting. Gordon noticed immediately the judge's eyes were red and irritated as if he had cried or was about to. Newell sat down, and wiped his eyes with a tissue.

"It's clear to me that she's in a better place. I have no hesitation in filing the adoption petition right now. If that is what you want?"

"Of course," said Miranda, looking at her husband, who also leaned forward, agreeing.

Newell pressed a button on his desk and said, "Missy, would you please bring in the paperwork on the Di Angelos to me?"

Missy answered back, "Yes. I'll be right in." Soon the big chamber doors opened, and Missy had a file folder in her hand. She laid it down on the desk in front of the judge.

"April, how about you go with Missy? She'll show you more books, and maybe give you a job." The judge smiled at April.

April happily followed Missy out of the room, and the door closed behind them. Judge Du Val looked at his friends, the Di Angelos, and said, "This is a tragedy and a miracle in one. I have no doubt this adoption will go through. Should anyone come forward and want her back, there's a boatload of abuse, including scars to back it all up. From the time we sign these papers today, in exactly two years she will legally be your daughter."

Miranda began to cry. It took a little while to regain her composure, and the judge told them what he asked of April. "I want her to come to you as her parents, but I also want her to come to me.

I can reinforce anything you want. Please let me do this. Let me be her uncle, of sorts, especially since I may never be a father myself. I know you can support her. But I can also, in a different way, as a guide should she need my help."

Gordon could only thank his friend.

"Okay. Now let's sign this before we forget," the judge said, and they laughed. The judge then called Missy back into the room for her signature as a witness. April came along wearing a paper hat Missy had made for her.

"Wow, you look like a pirate," Gordon said to her. April laughed and stood by his chair. "Well, April, since we're all friends here, I want you to know that one day these two will become your parents. And *I*"—he used both his hands to press at his chest—"*I* will be your uncle. So as you grow up, you will have not one, not two, but three people to help you. How does that sound?" Judge Newell De Val asked her.

"That sounds good, and I'll be there for all of you too," she said. "But there are actually four. I know that Jesus watches over me. If not, then I wouldn't be here. He has always listened to me and answered my prayers. Maybe not right away, but always when it was needed."

Their laugh was a bit somber. They couldn't know how prophetic this statement from this little girl would be.

The drive home was almost a celebration. Gordon Di Angelo hadn't felt this happy in a long, long time, and remarkably, he didn't realize it until he pulled over at the Bandit, the local outdoor ice cream parlor.

"I think we all should have an ice cream cone, honey. What do you say?" he asked.

"I say pecan," said Miranda.

April stood with her legs on each side of the hump in the back seat floorboard.

"Well, I'm having a double dip of chocolate fudge. What about you?" the sheriff said.

"I don't know," April said.

And Gordon replied, "How about we go inside and see what you might like?"

April waited for him to open the rear car door. She got out and reached for his hand. Inside, a kind woman showed April many, many barrels of ice cream with all sorts of flavors. April decided on green mint.

"Just one scoop," she said. She didn't want more than that in case she didn't like it. They all had their ice cream cones and napkins for dripping. As April looked around, Miranda nudged her husband's knee. Talking low in a whisper, she said, "I can't believe it. It's an answer to my prayers. I can barely be hopeful and believe it."

"I know," Gordon said. "But let's take this carefully and remember that our real celebration will be in two years at about this time."

"I can't wait," Miranda said. "No, I'm going to jump right in and enjoy her no matter what. She will not stay little. Time has a way of passing us by so quickly."

"You're right," Gordon said, "I can't tell you to guard your heart. If anyone deserves to be a mother, you do. All I can say is, do what you feel is right."

He held her hand as they sat and watched April take interest as the woman kept scooping ice cream for others. And that is how her new life began, with loving, caring guardians who enjoyed having her with them.

And, you know, life was pretty good. Preparing for school before school began, Miranda took April to be tested to see her grade average for placement. As she sat waiting, she picked up a magazine, paged a few of the pages, but she couldn't settle down. How she wished she could be in the room with April as she was being tested. But then, didn't most mothers feel like this before entering school for the first time? As April came out, Miranda thought the tester would reveal the results, but the door closed quite quickly.

Another mother sitting there spoke to Miranda. "Don't let that bother you," she said. "They send the results in the mail, and your child's grade placement will be on the paper as well."

Miranda thanked the woman and asked her what her name was. "Oh, forgive me. I'm Mrs. Diane Marshall. I live over the hill from you."

"Oh yes. I remember now," Miranda said.

"This is my son, Trevor. He's being tested for second grade. We were out of the country, and he missed a lot of first grade, so he had to be retested. What is your daughter's name?" Diane Marshall asked.

"Her name is April," Miranda replied, as the two children naturally gravitated to one another. The children chatted as did the mothers, and soon they were all heading back home.

In the parking lot, Trevor looked at his mother and said, "That's my girlfriend," and Mrs. Marshall smiled at him. Who knew what would happen in time?

The Marshalls had two sons. Trevor was with her, and Hugh was at home and was four years older. Often, she would pray for a girl her boys would one day marry. She hoped the girls her sons would marry would become friends with her, share recipes, go to the movies once in a while, take in a program, or go on a short trip together. And she sighed. Her mother-in-law wasn't around much, and then she'd passed away within the fourth year of their marriage. Then her father-in-law had followed his wife within two years. She'd liked her mother-in-law. But the truth was, they were never close. There was never time, and they lived so far away. She was still grateful to have her father who was now in his late sixties, and he was active, healthy and fairly fit for his age.

My New Life

Life for the Di Angelo family settled in as if it was meant to be. One day, the sheriff came home early for lunch and saw his wife and soon-to-be daughter singing and dancing to Mr. Rogers again. It was priceless. They didn't hear him come in, so he stood there watching them. To think that just a few days ago they were a married couple with a small farm and animals. They were living alone, almost independent, and now they were a family. The transition was so easy, like breathing. They were a family, not officially, but it sure felt like it.

They soon settled into a routine. Gordon, of course, went to work every day and served his community as their sheriff. His wife, Miranda, stayed at home with April, who began to have a routine of her own. In short order, April talked to her parents about having pony trail rides—charging children money to ride ponies. They could travel across their ranch and the meadows, up into the woods, around the back canyon, circling around then crossing the river, and then back home. It was easily a forty-five-minute ride.

On a Saturday morning after chores, the sheriff watched April saddle and tie each pony nose to tail. She spoke to each one and called them by name. She told them that they were going on an adventurous ride. April got on the lead pony, Dobbins, and they were off—all twenty-two of them in a row.

Gordon wanted so badly to go with her, to watch over her, but he had promised he wouldn't walk alongside her. But he didn't promise that he wouldn't take his own horse and ride along or behind. So that's what he did. In a little while, he easily caught up to the pack, and rode up beside her.

"How are they handling, April?" he asked. "Oh, fine. If only the end would stop swinging to be near the front. When they do that, I have to spur Dobbins on to stay in the lead," she said.

"Oh, I think when you have riders, they will keep their ponies in a line," Gordon reassured her.

Yes, that pony ride was ninety minutes long. The most frightening part was crossing the small river because not all the ponies were quite so sure. But as the first went in, each followed. Gordon was relieved when they were all back at the barn.

Methodically, she unsaddled each pony, leaving them tied by halters to the rail. Then she placed the saddles where they belonged, and the bridles were hung on the horn. She brushed down each pony and released them into the pasture. The grass was short, not lush, and the ponies would be all right.

"Are you tired out, pumpkin?" he asked his daughter.

"Nope, not at all. It was fun. I may have to change the lineup because Dobbins is slower than some of the others."

"I'd be patient. Dobbins likes you, and she handles well with you. She's the leader of the mares. I think when there are other riders, Dobbins will be assertive and take the lead no matter what," Gordon answered her.

"Yeah, you might be right," April said matter-of-factly.

"Oh, so you think so?" Gordon teased her. He got up and began to chase her.

April giggled as she ran, and she was determined to escape him. She darted around the trees and under the wash-line fence where Miranda was hanging wet laundry. It was so much fun. When he finally caught her, they were both out of breath. They hugged each other and laughed and laughed.

Miranda saw the chase and was thrilled inside. They were so happy. She wanted to share this happiness with all of their friends and family—but not just yet.

Yes, they all had a routine. Soon Miranda was outside every Saturday, telling people where to park their cars and vans. Children would come tumbling out. It was quite the scene. With each new group, Miranda would discover little changes that made this easier. By the time of the third weekend, things were running smoothly. The cars parked at the rails in a row. As the children arrived, the ponies were already saddled and waiting in a line on the opposite side. Children would stand by the pony they chose to ride. Each had to put on a helmet, as parents signed a waiver not to sue in the event of an injury. April would be first to mount, and would call for the others to mount their ponies. Miranda would open the gate, and soon the entire line of twenty-two ponies and their riders would pass her.

"Good luck and happy riding," she would call to the children as she waved.

There were cold drinks in the cooler that were given to them. And when they got back, Miranda would have hot dogs on a rolling grill and hot chicken barbecues waiting for hungry parents and children. April loved this. She was a born leader and loved all of the ponies and their riders. April was so helpful when someone was scared or unsure. This became quite a moneymaker for the family as well. Each rider only paid five dollars. When there were twenty-two riders, that came to $110. And there were three rides on Saturdays—$330, cha-ching! That easily fixed broken equipment.

Oftentimes, some of the ponies were sold. That would mean April and Gordon would have to go to auctions in search of other ponies. And it never failed, the supply was endless. It was nothing for them to come back with four to six more ponies. Some weren't so giving or trained, and that was a job April relished. She was a smart rider and could always trick the ponies into doing what she wanted.

"You have to outsmart them," she would say.

Well, this sure kept them busy. As fall approached, the annual horse and pony show was ramping up in town. April was determined to enter and compete. Gordon had purchased three larger ponies: one white, one flea gray, and a bay. April was on their backs more than she was in the house. They all had lovely gaits, and two of the three jumped. April intended to show the two and sell the white one. Or maybe all when they did well. Poppa also thought it was an excellent idea. Soon Miranda found herself sewing show costumes, and she was determined to make sure her daughter was seen. Many sequin beads were sewed into the shirts and sleeves. Miranda made belts as well, with many sparkles or bling, as the children would say.

April kept her word on the morning of the pony section of the show. April didn't have a chance to ride one of the mares. A mother wanted to buy the pony for her daughter to show on and keep. There were no tears. Indeed, April was happy and helpful, and clued the mother to the pony's traits and habits.

The mother was impressed, and her daughter did well, considering the girl hadn't ridden this pony more than on the trail rides at the Di Angelo's farm. Yes, it had all gone well. April rode the two mares in western pleasure, pleasure riding, and western trail. She placed first and second. The last mare, the bay, was a talented jumper, and April placed first.

Immediately after the show, the mayor of the town approached Miranda. He wanted to know the price for the bay. Miranda wasn't sure if April wanted to sell this mare, since she was new. The mayor insisted that his daughter had to have the pony, and soon Gordon was at Miranda's side. He put the mayor at ease, assuring him that they would speak to April about the bay, and be in touch with him by telephone.

As the show ended, the ponies that hadn't sold were loaded to go home. On the ride home, April's parents mentioned what the mayor had asked of them.

"Are you kidding me?" April said. "Vicky can't ride for crap. I could win on a horse, and if she rode the same horse, that mare wouldn't place."

Miranda was shocked at April's comments. "How can you be so mean, April? His daughter likes horses, and just needs to learn more to develop her skills," she said.

April replied, "No, some people have talent and can really ride. They like it, and they do well. His daughter rides for the attention of her parents. When she gets tired of it, she'll quit, and the mare will be left standing."

Gordon got it. He knew exactly what April was saying. Miranda didn't like it, but it was the truth.

So that summer, they learned that showing was on Saturdays only, not Sundays. If the shows fell on a Sunday, they didn't go. They wanted peace more than anything. This change was needed.

That was a huge change for the Di Angelos. Before April came, they used to lounge around on a Sunday, go visiting, for walks, or out for dinner. If they wanted to have a Christ-centered life, they knew they had to change. On Sundays, they were up at the crack of dawn to get their chores done, so they could leave home by eight thirty to get to church. But in truth, they loved it. They became closer friends with many in their own neighborhood and city.

As sheriff of the town, Gordon had respect, but he felt like a child at church. The teachings were simple and true, and he felt it in the core of his being. Seeing how much his daughter loved going and how she changed into such a kind, loving little girl, he would never think of returning to their old ways.

Miranda used to spend many lonely days at home. She knew in time, April would be off to school all day long, and she would sit at home alone. Oh, there were things to do, but she missed the bustle of family. There was a women's group called the Relief Society. It was full of forty or more young, middle-age, and older women. They sang songs and had a lesson. There were opportunities to visit one another, do crafts, and exchange recipes. Miranda found a way of true happiness through service to others. It was on a Sunday that a fellow neighbor came to them in the hallway while changing classes. He approached Gordon asking if they would be interested in a young bull calf that was struggling, not doing so well.

He had the farm animals for something to do. But now, working as a consultant, he was away often. He barely had time for the healthy cattle, let alone a sickly one. April pulled at her father's sleeve, looked at him with soulful eyes as if pleading.

"Okay, yes. Sure, we'll stop by later this afternoon and pick up the calf," replied Gordon. And that is how April's life began in a way no one ever expected. Every few weeks, a sick calf would arrive, and then another, and another. Soon they were up to fifteen calves. They decided to rent a farm adjacent to theirs. There were always bull calves available, inexpensive, but some sickly. April often took as many as she could take or pay for.

It only took ten minutes by foot, or four minutes if by four-wheeler, to take the calves grain and hay. Gordon was determined that next year they would have hay in place and a nice grain bin to make feeding more efficient. That was the year April began third grade—that was her test-out level. Miranda felt April would do better in fourth, but there was no sense in arguing. The school counselor assured Miranda that if April's test scores and maturity were enough, they could put her in fourth grade later on in the school year. Or they could retest her after this year and skip a grade if necessary.

Miranda was upset, she never heard of such a thing. It took her levelheaded husband to talk to her. "Sweetheart, whoever heard of someone picking a young girl off of the street and giving her a home. We aren't even sure of her birth year. Let it go. Let's see how she does this year and go from there."

Miranda put her hands down as she was folding towels.

"You're right again!" And she pouted at him.

Gordon stood up and kissed her lips. Pulling her face to his, he said to her, "Miranda Di Angelo, I love you more and more each day with each beat of my heart."

With that the front door banged open, making them both jump. April came in the door out of breath.

"That one bull calf is a dope. He loves to chase the others around, and he is going to be trouble. I think we need to put him by himself or castrate him really soon so he settles down. I checked his records, and he's seventeen weeks old. Maybe someone only castrated the one testicle, and the other one might be up inside. Because he isn't right."

Gordon came to her, and said, "Okay. We can have the vet come out this week and check him. Okay?"

"Nope, I can do it," April replied.

Gordon looked at her stunned, "April, this is a fairly good-sized calf. He can easily knock you down, and I don't want you getting hurt."

"Oh, I won't get hurt, if you do your part right," she said.

Gordon should have known she knew what she was doing. And she was determined to get it done. So off the three of them went with a rope, surgical scissor, and iodine. The ride on the four-wheeler was fun—it was always fun. Gordon loved that his family was all together. Miranda sat behind him looking all around. She loved the outdoors. As a child, she explored so much of her family's ranch. But now, she was inside most of the time unless helping April with the pony rides.

Soon they were at the barn. There were twelve calves on each side, a total of twenty-four calves in all, the older, bigger calves on one side, and the younger, smaller ones on the other. The crazy one was easy to spot. He was bumping others with his head, pushing them. He would bulldog them into the side of the pen, and the weaker ones would fall down.

Gordon stood on the rail and lassoed the calf. He let the line loose and climbed into the pen.

"You be careful, Gordon," his wife called. Gordon didn't answer her.

The calf, out of curiosity, came toward him. But soon the calf's head was down, and he was coming after Gordon. He quickly moved to one side, and the calf passed him. As the calf passed, Gordon pulled the rope as hard as he could, and the calf fell down. Gordon put the rope in a calf halter and tied the calf to the post.

Then April came in the pen with oversized blue surgical gloves, the scissor, and iodine. She lifted the one leg of the calf, pushing him as hard as she could, and the calf fell over onto its side.

"Can you hold the one leg for me?" she asked. April quickly made a one-inch incision on the scrotum and fished out a fairly good-sized testicle. It had fastened itself up inside the bull calf. April put her fingers around the adhesions of the testicle and pulled hard. As she stood up, her hand held the bloody testicle. Then she dropped it onto the straw bedding and doused the calf's scrotum to ward off infection.

"No stitches?" asked Miranda.

"No. He will be fine. There are no others that are nasty like he was. The pen is clean and dry, so he should be all right."

By the time school began, the steer count was up to sixty-five calves. The rental barn was full, and there was no room to put any more. The hay mow was full, as were the three-ton feed bins—one for cracked corn and the other for calf feed. The automatic waterer still worked well.

Gordon wondered if Mrs. Adams's pastures would be available and how the fencing was. He remembered that last year there were two horses that used the pastures. So he stopped by her house one day on his rounds, and asked.

Mrs. Adams was elderly, and didn't want the horse people back. "They never paid me for the rent," she said. And she knew the sheriff to be an honest man and that seeing the sheriff out here may deter others from bothering her. So it was agreed—the Di Angelos would rent the barn for twenty dollars a month. It was their responsibility to keep it up and clean. The pastures for ten dollars a month. After all, the animals would keep the grass and weeds down, and the land would look better. And she liked seeing the animals out there, since she grew up on this dairy farm and missed seeing the cows.

Out of gratitude for her kindness in allowing them to rent the barn and pastures, Miranda often baked or brought a dinner to her. In time, they struck up quite a good friendship. Mrs. Adams thought of Miranda as her daughter, and April was, well, the sweetest little thing ever. She picked her flowers, brought her candy, talked about the animals. She always asked what it was like when she was a little girl. And her company was priceless.

Many people were curious to know how April was so successful raising calves. If they were sick, she kept them separate, all alone on dry bedding. She hydrated them with special formula, and kept them on raw cow's milk as best as she could. As they progressed, she put them on milk replacer. It was rare for her to ever use antibiotics. She found that when she did, they didn't make it anyway. Yes, she had losses, but her time with the calves was invaluable. April found that often they wanted attention. Sometimes just sitting with a sick calf, rubbing them, made all the difference in the world.

Not all the calves were as sick as others. They didn't understand drinking on a bottle, and they headbutted until they were weak. With those, she kept a very small-holed nipple, so they had to learn how to suck. For others, there was always a trick, each calf was different. They truly had personalities all their own, just like people. With consistency, the ones that survived did well. At one point there were twenty-two calves on milk, but there were only ten buckets. They had to take turns, and babies all want to drink right now.

April had to know who drank and who did not. To solve that,

she put food color in the buckets. Once they drank, they had that color on their mouths, and she knew. In time, they did learn to take turns. It takes six weeks to keep a calf on milk, six long weeks. April made sure to get them drinking from a bucket as soon as she could. Once they drank out of a bucket, they would eat grain and hay sooner and grow.

One harsh lesson she learned was that newborn calves should have their own mother's milk. A newborn calf, either a bull (boy) or a heifer (girl), has four stomachs, and the mother cow has DNA in her milk. That DNA seals the gaps in the babies' stomachs. If no DNA, April found that those calves didn't do as well. They would develop diarrhea, and then it was a battle to save them. Yes, April was a worker, and took on this challenge with joy.

Mrs. Adams had a great-grandson, Brock. He was nothing like April. Brock was a spoiled boy. His father liked to drink, and she was fearful Brock would turn out just like his father. Brock was always in trouble. It seemed like he was angry all the time. Whenever Brock was near the Adam's farm, April either wasn't there or left in a hurry.

So that fall, as school began, April was entering third grade. She and Miranda sometimes had a struggle with what to wear to school. Miranda wanted April to wear a dress and pretty shoes. April wanted to wear colorful jeans and a shirt with sneakers. So a deal was reached. On Wednesdays it was dress up day. The rest of the time, April could wear, with Mother's approval, what she wanted.

The pony rides continued, and so did April's want for more calves, or cows. Mrs. Adams told April all about milking. April must have felt yearning for her old home life, as she kept asking if she could get some milk cows.

"What in heaven's name for?" her daddy asked.

"To make money, of course," she replied.

"Money? You will have to work every day, twice a day milking cows. Never a day off, not ever. Not when you are sick. Not when you want to go visit or go to church. Christmas, Easter, your birthday, every single day of the year, you will have to milk cows—twice a day. Is that what you want?" he asked.

"Yes. I do," was her defiant answer.

But with school beginning, there were new faces, new things to do and learn. So, for now, he could keep her at bay. There was no way Gordon Di Angelo, or his wife, wanted a career of milking cows.

April never complained. On school mornings, she was usually up by 5:00 a.m. and finished with the ponies by six. Then she rode the four-wheeler to the Adams's barn and fed the steers grain and hay, sometimes giving them straw for fresh bedding. She would be back home by six forty-five, in time to see her daddy and give him a kiss goodbye as he left for work. If she was earlier, they would have breakfast together.

Often, she dressed downstairs, holding onto Ruby. The dog was absolutely, completely spellbound by anything April did. Ruby was an elderly dog that the Di Angelos had gotten from the pound shortly before April came to live with them. When Gordon saw her, he felt an outpouring of love. He felt that this little lost soul needed someone to care for her, and his wife would be happy.

Eh? Not so much. Miranda liked the dog. She fed her and let her in and out. But the dog would never have been her choice. She was happy that April loved the dog, and Ruby responded to April's every call and demand. They were best buds at bath and bedtime.

By seven thirty, the bus would arrive at their driveway. April was usually waiting, watching for it as it came down the road in the darkness of early morning. She went out the door before the bus stopped, always stopping to kiss her mom on the cheek.

As she ran out of the door, her mom would always holler to her, "Remember who you are."

April was to reply, "I know. God doesn't make junk. I'm a child of God." That always put a big smile on Miranda's face.

School was great, and April loved it. She had many friends, both boys and girls. As the months rolled on, the school was gearing up for a holiday event at Christmas time. You could sign up for anything on your own or with a group—singing or dancing. April had learned to tap dance at her home far away. She asked Miranda what she should do for the talent portion.

"Do you know how to play any musical instrument, like maybe a guitar?" Miranda asked her.

"No, I don't," April replied.

"Well, I know that Gordon loves to play his guitar, and I'm sure he would teach you, if you asked him."

That very night when Gordon came home for supper, April was already asking hundreds of questions about how to play a guitar. After dinner, Gordon came downstairs with a guitar. It was big, but he showed April how to hold the guitar and to strum chords. It seemed all too easy for her. She loved it, and in just a short time, she was playing a little song. Gordon was thrilled. He loved to play and used to play a lot. Now he had someone who loved something he did.

The next day, they chose a song for her to play at the Christmas pageant. They chose "Silent Night." It was her daddy's favorite Christmas song, and he wanted his daughter to know why. So one evening, as they sat together as a family, he brought forth a book—the true story of how the most beloved Christmas song came to be:

The True Story of Silent Night. Her daddy sat down and told her about how this song came to be written down.

On Christmas Eve in 1818, in the little Alpine village of Oberndorf in northern Austria, it was snowing hard. The people of the little town had long before gone to bed, and all was quiet and still. But there was one light still burning. It shone from the study window of the young priest, Joseph Mohr.

Joseph Mohr hadn't been able to go to sleep that night. He had been pacing up and down his study, pausing now and then to look out of the window at the silent, snow-covered scene before him. He was deeply worried. Christmas, a day of music and rejoicing, was almost here. As yet, he had seen no way to overcome the disappointment he knew was in store for his congregation. The truth of the matter was that the church organ was in bad need of repair, and there was no repairman in the town of Oberndorf. And the heavy snows had made it impossible to get one from anywhere else.

He was thinking of this and, at the same time, remembering a conversation he had the preceding summer with his friend Frans Gruber. Gruber was a school teacher in the town of Arnsdorf, not far away. Gruber was also an accomplished musician and played the organ in the village church. One day, they were sitting in the pastor's garden singing together to the accompaniment of Gruber's guitar. Suddenly, Gruber had stopped in the middle of a hymn and turned to his friend.

"Father," he said, "do you realize that none of these Christmas songs we've been singing expresses the real Christmas spirit?"

"You are right, my friend," the priest answered.

"Perhaps one day someone will write a song that will tell simply the meaning of Holy Night."

"Why should not that someone be you?" asked the schoolmaster.

Joseph Mohr had laughed. "And will you write the music, if I do?"

"Of course," Gruber replied. "And I'm quite serious about this. I'm sure you can do it."

In the weeks that followed this conversation, Joseph Mohr had tried to write that song. But somehow, try as he might, the words simply didn't come. And now it was Christmas Eve. He felt a little sad as he thought of the service the next evening with no organ. And there was no new song to sing to his people as he had planned.

As he stood at his window, lost in thought, he suddenly realized that someone was struggling through the deep snow toward his house. He rushed to the door and went out to help his exhausted visitor into the warmth of his fire. It was a woman, too breathless to speak for some moments, but at last, she was able to tell her story. She had come over the mountain from the cabin of a friend of hers who that night had given birth to her first child, a son.

"And, Father," the woman concluded, "her husband, who is a young woodcutter, is very anxious that you come and bless the new mother and babe this very night."

"Of course, I'll go," the priest answered.

"But the snow is getting very deep now," the woman protested. "I came as I promised him I would, but I'm sure he'll understand if you wait until morning. T'was not snowing hard like this when I left their house."

"I don't mind the snow, and the walk will be good for me," Joseph

Mohr answered. "I'm feeling too wakeful to go to bed anyway. You stay here until you're rested before you go home."

Bundling himself up in his warmest clothes and taking a stout cane to help him, the priest started out. It was several miles to the woodcutter's cabin, and the heavy snow made it difficult to walk. When he arrived and opened the door, he caught his breath at the scene before him. It was one he would never forget.

There was the new mother in her bed, smiling happily at her husband, who was kneeling in adoration before a crude wooden crib in which lay his newborn son. It seemed to Joseph Mohr that he was looking at a scene that had taken place in Bethlehem of Judea many ages before.

The young woodcutter felt the sudden draft of cold air, and rose quickly to his feet. "Welcome, Father," he cried. "I didn't expect you to come when I realized how hard it was snowing. But I'm grateful you're here."

Proudly, he led the priest over to the cradle where the child lay, and Father Mohr admired the baby. Then he gave the child and mother his blessing. Although the woodcutter wanted the priest to partake of some refreshment before he left, Father Mohr replied that he must be on his way.

Bidding goodbye to the happy parents, he set out for home. This time, the way didn't seem quite so hard. The snow was no longer falling, but the branches of the pine trees bent low under their heavy white mantel. The stillness in the forest was awe-inspiring. As he plowed through the drifts, the pastor kept thinking of the little family he had just left. Truly, this had been a holy night.

At home, he could hardly wait to take off his coat and warm his stiff fingers. Then he sat down at his desk and began to write. It was early morning before he finished, and he fell exhausted upon his bed for a little rest. But he didn't stay there long. Soon he arose, ate his breakfast, and hurried out again. This time he went in the direction of Arnsdorf, where his friend Franz Gruber lived. When Gruber opened his door, Joseph Mohr handed him the manuscript containing the words he had written in the early morning hours.

"My friend," the priest said, "here is the new Christmas song. Will you set it to music as you once promised?"

Franz Gruber's eyes shone as he read the beautiful verses. Grasping the pastor's hand, he said, "I shall do my best, and we'll sing it at the services tonight. My guitar will be our accompaniment."

That evening the congregation gathered in the little church at Oberndorf to hear their priest preach his Christmas sermon. After he had finished telling them the meaning of the Star in Bethlehem, Franz Gruber came and stood with him. The altar candles cast a soft glow around them as together they sang the hymn that combined talents had produced.

As the last words, "Christ the Savior is born," were heard, the people in this little church were filled with a reverence they hadn't known before. They couldn't have imagined that they were having the privilege of hearing for the first time, a song that, in years to come, would be the best loved of Christmas carols.

The weather turned cold, unusually cold for Fresno, California, that year. The temperature dipped below freezing, and everyone was complaining. The forecast didn't look like the freezing was going to lose its grip anytime soon. If the rain drizzled, the roads would slightly freeze, and the fog was always a concern.

On one evening, Gordon came home with a heavy heart. A man they had known in the community for a long time had an accident on the slippery roads in the fog, hit a tree, and died.

The family had two sons and a daughter. That daughter was a good friend of April's. And they didn't know how to tell April, so they didn't. The Christmas pageant was in a few weeks, so the Di Angelos thought they would wait until after that. In the meantime, they would take care of the family with meals and needs they would have.

The Pageant

APRIL WAS READY AND PRACTICED her guitar playing all the time. She sang "Silent Night" every chance she could. Her parents were patient and tried to be calm, but April playing that song over and over was getting to them. April wasn't interested in anything but one doll for Christmas that she had seen in a catalog flier. Both Miranda and Gordon went hunting in various stores to find it, but couldn't find one. Their house was full of Christmas décor. The stair rail had greenery, and they put up a nice Christmas tree with a lot of ornaments. Stockings were put up by the old fireplace in the parlor room. It was all so pretty and exciting.

They took a trip together to a big department store. There in the store was a huge display with stuffed reindeer, elves, and Santa Claus sitting on a chair. April felt that if she could tell Santa, it would all work out. For some reason, she felt he wasn't the real Santa. He smelled funny, and, well, she did sit on his lap to tell him what she had hoped for. And all he said was, "Ah, hem. Well."

The whole week before the pageant, April had chores like all children. On one Saturday after her chores outside, April started vacuuming upstairs as her mother asked.

She went from room to room with the vacuum cleaner humming. At one door, April knew this was a closet, but it too had carpeting. So she opened the door and began to vacuum that rug.

April saw a big brown shopping bag with the name of the department store they had been to a few days before. She knew she should not peek inside, but she did. There on top was the doll she had been hoping for. Her breath caught, and it was very hard for her to hide her delight. She felt guilty because she knew, but her heart danced with joy. In the days that followed, some older kids talked about Santa coming to the school when the closing announcements were made. April wasn't so sure about that. Those kids were much older than she was, and maybe, just maybe, they knew.

The truth was, parents purchased a toy and wrapped it up. Then they put their child's name on the package to ensure their child would get that gift. They were instructed to drop their package off at the school office. The day of the Christmas pageant came, and the wind swirled. There were even snowflakes. Imagine: flurry snowflakes! When the wind blew in your face, it would sting. It was a surprise winter that adults hated, and children hoped for. It seemed like there was magic in the air.

Miranda had already laid out April's clothing for the evening pageant that Friday when April came home from school. April put her book bag in her room on the floor and changed into her barn clothing, then took care of the calves and ponies. She was back in the house before her dad came home from work. They quickly had some soup and a sandwich. Then they all washed and dressed to go to the pageant. Gordon carried April's guitar. Once there, it was like a dream. All of the little friends together, no lines. The parents were all packed into the gym on chairs. It was so exciting. The lights went dim and bright again. That was a signal to quiet the crowd. The principal came to the center of the stage to give the announcements—reading off the program each person had been given as they entered the school.

And then it began: the plays, singing, individual acts of juggling, dancing, and playing instruments. It was obviously pleasing the parents, which was evident by the smiles on their faces. When the pageant was over, the principal came out onto the stage again to thank the children and their parents. And reminded them to be careful, and drive home safely. He gave a brief overview of the weather.

As the parents stood up to put on their coats, most of the children stayed, glued to their seats. And, sure enough, Santa Claus came into the side door of the gym, ringing bells, saying, "Ho, ho, ho, merry Christmas." He looked an awful lot like the janitor.

There was a flurry of children running to him. It was noisy, and parents were standing. April couldn't see. Then her mother touched her shoulder and motioned for her to go forward. She was in no hurry.

There was a huge gathering of children around a big red bag and Santa. It was curious to April that the school secretary was helping Santa, and she quickly realized that the school secretary knew him.

April just stood there. One by one, a child's name would be called, and Santa would hand them a package. Then they would run excitedly to their parents to show them what they got.

April knew what she wanted. She began to hold her breath, waiting for her name to be called. One package after another, and she stood there waiting.

Then, almost at the bottom of the bag, Santa picked up a package and called April's name. She took the package and held on to it tightly. She didn't need to rip open the paper because she was holding onto the very thing she wanted most.

And then, as April walked away, loud crying brought April to reality. She saw her little friend crying. There were no more presents left in that big red bag.

Santa tried to console her by giving her candy canes, and the school secretary was giving her dollar bills. But nothing stopped those tears. She didn't understand why she didn't get a gift from Santa.

Seeing her dear friend cry with deep, sobbing breaths, April felt something inside her that made her heart leap. April placed her hand over her name tag, carefully tearing it off. Then she walked back to that red bag and Santa. She said, "Look, there was a mistake. I got your present instead of mine."

April handed her little friend her package. The young girl stopped crying immediately and went scampering off to find her mother. April turned to go back to her parents. It was Miranda Di Angelo who found April empty handed with eyes welling with tears.

Miranda scooped her daughter up into her arms, burying her head to April's ear saying over and over. "I'm so very proud of you."

This wasn't planned by parents, but by a loving, kind Father in Heaven. April's little friend was the daughter of the man who had died in the accident. April hadn't been told, but inside she knew her friend needed something, for there was no happiness in her.

There never was, nor ever would be, another dolly like that for April. She would never ask for another. Miranda and Gordon followed suit, and that grieving family had one of the nicest Christmases ever. It was complete with gifts and a full meal with all the trimmings, right down to the sticks of butter.

The Di Angelos had a simple meal of scrambled eggs and ham, and they were happy. There were games to play, time to be shared, and at the end of that day, the Di Angelos were happier with less than ever before. It was a valuable lesson at a tender age that changed April forever. In time, she would grow through adversity. She would accept challenges that came to her, learn to handle them in a kinder way, and always seek God first. April had learned early in life that kindness mattered. Her own family, her own flesh and blood, would never have lifted a finger for the little friend. But she felt her biological mother would have, and she knew Miranda and Gordon would as well. There is nothing as lovely or delightful as a kind heart. And in time, others would learn of her kindness and tenacity.

Spring

FOURTH GRADE AND THE SEASONS flew by. By springtime, the pastures were all repaired, and there were fifty-four feeder steers grazing on Mrs. Adams's pastures. There were more in another field that was part grass pasture and part woods. There were Angus, Holstein, crossbreds, all sorts and sizes, and all steers for market. The pony rides continued. The guitar playing continued. Finding more sickly calves or good deals always ended back in the barn at Mrs. Adams. It was a real ranch by the time summer was in full swing. April was full steam ahead in all she did. Miranda Di Angelo was amazed at how much their lives had changed in the two years that April had been blessed to be with them. They were richer by far, materially and spiritually.

Soon they would make an appointment with the judge to finalize April's adoption, and she hoped that there would be no contesting to that finalization. She sighed and went into the house. It was Friday, and they were going out for supper at Flo's Diner. It sure was nice to be able to go out every once in a while as a family and see their neighbors.

When Gordon came home, the last of the riders were putting their ponies out on the lot. The day was done, the kids and ponies looked tired. Twenty-two riders and one straggling April.

"Boy, you're in the money today," Gordon said to her squeezing her shoulder with his strong hand.

April looked up at him and smiled. She held on to his strong hand as they said goodbye to the kids and their parents. As they walked into the house, Gordon handed April a pamphlet. It told about a county fair that was going on in June. There were all kinds of shows, contests and events.

"Can we go?" asked April.

"Sure, we can," Gordon said. "Your momma loves to go."

"Go where?" asked Miranda. Then she saw the flier, and made a face, but said nothing. If her daughter wanted to go, they would go, but she would rather stay home. The fair was a busy and sometimes dangerous place.

"Okay. Have the calves been fed?" Gordon asked.

"No," said April. "We just got back, and I can go now."

"Well, may I come along with you?" he asked his daughter.

April smiled at him, and they both walked toward the shed for the four-wheeler. April sat on the back while her Poppa rode steadily and carefully across the driveway. They went behind the barn, across the stream, and up over the hillside, taking in the beauty of the land. This was the long way around, but a nice way to destress after a long day at work.

The ride came to an end at Mrs. Adam's barn. And inside Gordon was amazed, again, that already April had accumulated twenty-eight calves. He said nothing, but didn't know what to do when the winter months would come. Not all would have to go in, but the little ones would, and how many more did she plan to get?

On the ride home, Gordon mentioned this to April. She slapped at his back, and told him not to worry. She was working on it. And she sure was. To the left of the Adams's farm was an abandoned farm. It was deep in a wooded area, and the land hadn't been farmed in years. There were snakes in the pond. And it was said that two brothers had an accident and died in the barn. No one went there, no one except April. She would explore there, the fallen-down buildings and the barn full of old dusty hay. It was interesting and spooky.

April felt the pastures could be fixed up. If the grass around the pond was mowed or trimmed, the snakes would leave. So that is what she began to do on her off time—on her own. She struggled loading the weed trimmer onto the four-wheeler with a gas can tied onto one side. But she did it and began the weeding. The only snakes she saw were black ones. She would scream, and the snake would leave, then she would keep working. She knew they meant no harm. They bite out of fear, so let them alone.

In just a matter of days, everything began to look nicer. The grass around all the trees was trimmed, and the fence line was moderately repaired with odds and ends of wire the Di Angelos had saved.

So, April took it upon herself to approach the owner of the farm one day after school. He lived in town in an apartment by himself. Mr. Earl James was very elderly and said to be mean. April didn't care. This was business, and she wanted Mr. Earl James to know what her plans were. April did tell her parents her plans, and her father's eyebrows went up a bit. Gordon Di Angelo knew Mr. Earl James well. He was a hardworking man. He was a good man who had been cheated by many because of his kindness and trusting nature.

Mr. Earl James was of strong character. He was a man of color who earned his way in life by never taking from anyone. He was always jovial and happy, that is, until later in life when he almost lost everything to the two swindling brothers, who did indeed lose their lives in that barn in a drunken fight with each other.

Gordon thought it would be good for April to learn about Mr. Earl James. He was a good teacher, a wise man, and he loved children. He never was blessed with children of his own. So Gordon's good nature took over, and he encouraged his daughter to indeed talk with Mr. James. But he would like to escort her. He promised, he wouldn't say much, but rather listen. As long as she promised to listen to Mr. James.

Miranda said nothing. She knew her husband had April's best interest at heart. And it was good for April to learn about all people of the earth, every culture, every creed and race. All men were created in the image of God, and we all needed to help each other along.

It was planned that Gordon would make the appointment. Then he would pick up April at school on the appointed day, and both of them would go to Mr. Earl James together. It was now the end of March. Spring was beginning to show everywhere. The appointment with Mr. Earl James was for Thursday. Miranda baked Irish soda bread knowing this man was part Irish, and a kind gesture never hurt.

Gordon drove to James's apartment. They got out of the truck, and went up the steps. They pushed the doorbell button. *Bzzzzzzz*, the loud busser made a noise. Soon there appeared a very neatly dressed black woman at the door. She had on a light blue dress with a white pinafore apron. April knew Miss Annabelle very well since this woman served lunches at the school. She had the softest smile, soft kind hands, and the brightest eyes. April liked Miss Annabelle very much.

"Hello, Miss Annabelle," April said. "How are you?"

Miss Annabelle answered with a smile, "Fine. Fine. I'm just fine."

"We came to speak with Mr. Earl James, and have an appointment," April told her.

"Why, yes. I know that, and Mr. James is in the parlor just waiting for you. How about you and your daddy follow me, and then I'll bring in some nice lemonade."

"Oh, that would be just great, Miss Annabelle," Gordon said.

Gordon Di Angelo had known Annabelle since she was a little girl. She came to Fresno when she was about six with two of her brothers and an aunt. Her momma had tuberculosis and signed herself into an asylum, never to come out again. The girl had a hard life of labor, in homes and in factories. A small fraction of the community raised money for Annabelle to attend a school for culinary arts. Upon graduation with honors, Annabelle left for New York, got her degree, and came back home.

Yes, Fresno was home to Miss Annabelle. Her family was all gone now, and she found refuge with Mr. Earl James who was like a father to her. She loved her job in the school. It gave her the opportunity to be around children, since she wasn't married, and had none of her own, which she regretted.

So the Di Angelos, Gordon and April, went into the parlor room to see Mr. James while Annabelle disappeared into the big apartment. Mr. James tried to stand as they came into the room. Gordon Di Angelo trotted toward the big man to steady him. He took his hand, looked directly in the big man's face, and steadied him with his other hand on his shoulder.

"It's all right, Earl. We aren't royalty," Gordon said, and both men laughed.

Gordon pulled up a straight chair right beside Mr. James and sat down. April sat in front of Mr. James on a round green-colored foot stool. April stood as the man was seated and walked to him to shake his hand. April did that to introduce herself. Mr. James kissed the back of her hand. April didn't pull her hand away. Instead, she bowed her head as if in gratitude of a new friend.

They sat and talked. April made clear, leaving nothing hidden, her plans for Mr. James's farm. Mr. James looked at Gordon from time to time with wide wild eyes.

"She has plans." Mr. James laughingly said.

"Oh. Yes, she does," answered Gordon.

So, during that half hour, plans were made. There were handshakes to seal the deal to use the pastures at his farm, nothing more.

"No rent required, just take care of the land," he said to them.

April thanked Mr. James as they had their delicious lemonade, and said, "Mr. James, you do know that in time I'm going to buy that farm from you. It just makes sense. I love farms, and I love to work. And I'll buy it from you for a fair price, because I know you don't want the city to have it. I know you don't want your land developed for homes. And I'll bring you the best beef you ever tasted," April said.

Mr. James just nodded. And then Mr. James made a sort of sweeping motion with his one very aged, spotted hand for Miss Annabelle to take April away. Miss Annabelle understood and asked April if she would like to come with her to see the myna bird that Mr. James had for a pet. And of course, she did.

When they left, Mr. James spoke frankly with Gordon Di Angelo, and Gordon had to answer honestly. That this last piece of conversation had never been part of the plan when he made the appointment. April had ideas of her own and often didn't discuss them with him or his wife.

Mr. James sat there like a Cheshire cat, smiling. He liked that about the little girl. Already she was brutally blunt and could throw down the truth weather you liked it or not. Honesty is a rare, sought-after trait, and he hoped she would never lose it. Sometimes people can be so greedy and cruel that it can change a person. It did him. But now he felt hopeful. Now he felt inspired to go out and see his land.

Lord, he hadn't been out there in over forty years. The thought of it would anger him, but now, now he had good reason to go. He thought of it as a healing. And if it worked out, of course he would sell it to this little girl. Who would want it more? Who would take care of it?

April came back, full of enthusiasm about the new pet she just spent time with. It was time to leave, and without hesitation or reserve April threw her arms around Mr. James's neck and kissed his weathered cheek.

"Goodbye, Mr. James. It was sure nice to finally meet you. I hope you will come out and visit us, and come and see what I did on your land."

Mr. James was a little taken aback. No one had hugged him in years, but you know, it was nice. It sure was nice.

That spring there was a lot to happen: the adoption finalization, selling feeder steers, or raising them until finished. She was gearing up for the spring rides with the ponies. There were now over thirty of them, and April talked about having a pony sale.

Miranda, in her good-natured way, loved it all. She had never seen her life this way, but she loved it. She absolutely loved it.

Soon April was making fliers to be copied and displayed in stores and at bead boards around town. The sale was to be held the first Saturday in April. The ponies were all lined up, fully tacked. Riders had a chance to have ridden them before, or could do it now in the big riding ring. Miranda stationed herself behind a table with paper and pens. There were contracts in the filing cabinet beside her, which also held many of the pony's registrations. There were hot dogs on the rolling grill, with a bun warmer. There was a condiment table with everything imaginable, and cold sodas and bottled water in the extra refrigerator. Gordon brought home twelve-dozen doughnut boxes of all varieties for the customers to enjoy! It was going to be a busy day.

And they came. Word was out. By nine o'clock, there were eleven cars, some with small trailers, already lined up at their road. Kids were riding ponies in the ring, and some on their driveway. As children made their choices, often with their parents, one or both parents would go to Miranda to make the contract deal and pay for their purchase. Some had small trailers, some had horse trailers, and some paid a hauler to take their pony home for them. This went on until six o'clock.

Both of April's parents tried to assist her as she darted here and there. She helped kids choose a pony while helping them up, on, and off. By five, most of the crowd had dwindled to two or three looking at what was left. For the most part, the rush was over, and all three of the Di Angelos were tired. As Miranda was putting all the receipts into her portfolio bag, she went to go into the house. Then, in the driveway, came the mayor. He was puffing, and asked for April or Gordon.

"Why they were here a few minutes ago. They may have gone

feeding the steers. Wait here, and I'll call to them." Miranda suspected trouble, and she wanted to give her husband a heads-up.

As it was, both April and Gordon were in the house. Miranda pulled her husband aside, and told him who was there. Gordon looked up and out the window, and saw the mayor standing there by his station wagon. He was looking all around.

Gordon sighed, looking at his daughter, "Do you want to sell that flea-bitten mare or the bay to his daughter or not?"

April stood there shaking her head no.

"Well, this ought to be interesting," Gordon said, and he went out the door.

"Hello, Mayor Greely. How are you?" Gordon said cheerfully.

"I can tell you how I am. I want the bay for my daughter, Victoria. I asked last summer, and I have waited. I didn't know about this sale. I hope you have been honest with me, because I hate to disappoint my little girl. Tell me you didn't sell the bay." he said wiping his brow.

"No, she isn't sold, and we aren't selling her," Gordon said to him.

The mayor was astounded. He was sure that, since this was a sale of ponies, the bay or flea gray would also be in the sale.

"I hate to disappoint you, sir, but both of those ponies were bought with money that April earned herself, giving pony rides. They are outright hers. If she doesn't want to sell them, I can't make her—no more than you can make your daughter Victoria, not want."

April was soon at her father's side, but the mayor didn't notice her. She spoke up to him. "If you really want one of the ponies, I'll sell you the bay."

The mayor's eyes lit up, and it was obvious he was very excited.

"But she isn't going cheap. I'm going to ask $4,500 for her because she's worth every penny."

Both Gordon and the mayor just stared at April. Gordon was smiling, and the mayor was in disbelief. Gordon felt April could hold her own. She was playing hardball with the mayor, and he deserved it for his bullying ways.

"That's preposterous, and you know it." the mayor shouted out.

"Yes. It may be to you, but to your daughter, Vicky, who has no value of money, it's not. So that's the price for the very well-trained bay, $4,500."

The mayor stood there thinking for a moment, then reached into his pocket for a checkbook, and wrote out a check for $4,500. He handed the check to Gordon Di Angelo, who took that check, and handed it to April.

"Deliver the bay to our home on Monday. We need time to ready a stall," the mayor said as he got into his station wagon and sped out of the driveway.

"Boy, oh boy. He thinks he is special," April said.

"Yes, he does," said her father. "He is used to people doing what he wants. He's been mayor for over thirty-five years. No one opposes him. It isn't his experience that keeps him in office; it's his name. His father served as mayor, and he was a good honest man."

So, as they walked into their home, Miranda held out her hand for the check and fished out the papers for the bay mare. They were all too tired to go out to eat, so they sat down and had what was left over from the sale day. April was so tired she almost fell asleep at the table.

Gordon nudged his daughter and told her to go upstairs, wash, and then go to bed. April said she hadn't fed the calves yet, and her father simply said, "Go on. I'll do it." She never protested. She didn't even remember how she got upstairs or if she washed. But she was certainly asleep before the daylight fell.

As Gordon came back from feeding the calves, he looked into the pony pen. There was the bay, the flea gray, and three other ponies. That was all that was left. April was quite a salesperson, and they would need to go to the sale this week to replenish the riding ponies.

As he walked up the steps to his home and entered, Miranda was at the table with the expense sheets. She looked at him with tears in her eyes, saying. "Come look at this." Gordon looked over his wife's shoulder, and there in the last column was the grand total of sales—$77,000. That was almost equal to what Gordon Di Angelo made in a year as sheriff of the town, and they were astounded.

The portfolio was carefully put away, safely out of sight. The two of them went up to retire for the night. They both lay there together, wanting to talk. They talked about how well it had gone, the amount of money April made, not only at this sale, but also daily on pony rides that paid for all the calf feed and ponies they bought at the sales. April was living independently, earning her way. They were impressed, and a little troubled.

Miranda looked at her husband, "I think it is time we get away for a little while. I would like very much for April to come to my home in Mexico. I wanted to wait until she was surely ours, and soon she will be. Honey, I want to go home with her for my family to meet and know her."

Gordon lay there in the dark and sighed. He didn't mind going, but he knew he wasn't accepted by his wife's family. Tolerated at most. He was considered a gringo, not worthy of Mexican royalty.

He put his arm under his wife's head, and said, "When school is out, I can take some time off. We can make it a vacation, if you like," and she hugged him closer to her.

Gordon stroked her hair and mentioned that they needed to be thinking about a birthday of some sort for April. Her birthday was in April, and that was in a matter of days. Miranda hadn't forgotten, but the time was approaching so fast. They had busy lives, and April was like a whirlwind.

"How about we go to the lake for a day? I know April would like that," she said to her husband. "We can make it a picnic birthday. I know Mrs. Marshall goes up to the lake a lot. I believe her father lives there. And her youngest son, Trevor, is in the same class as April. He likes our daughter an awful lot. You know them? I know you do," she said in an asking way.

Gordon was on the brink of sleep, and said, "Yes. I know them well. Let's sleep on it, and talk about it in the morning on the way to church—or after. Okay?" and soon he was out.

Miranda lay there, thinking and thinking. Yes, she would call Mrs. Marshall tomorrow to make arrangements for their children to play and swim at the lake. She could make fried chicken with salads. They go easy. Andm well, she would make the call tomorrow. Plans are easier made with more than one person helping.

On the way home from church, the Di Angelos asked April about a picnic for her birthday. They could go to the lake and swim, picnic, and maybe a boat ride. As they rode along, Miranda wanted to stop to see someone that she didn't see at church. It would only take a minute. Gordon shut off the car. As they sat there, April pulled on his sleeve to look to the right where there was a brick double home listed for sale. Gordon looked at it, and it was in very good shape, at least from the outside.

"I think we should buy that, Dad," April said.

"What for? Why should I buy that double brick home?" he asked.

"Well, it would make a good rental. The people would pay the mortgage and taxes, and it would be a good income over the years," she answered.

Gordon looked at his daughter in disbelief. "What? How do you know about things like this?" he asked her.

"Because my grandpa did that, and he had a nice comfortable living when he retired from farming. The people who rented from him always paid," she answered.

Soon Miranda rejoined them in the car. She was full of a story from the people who had been sick and unable to attend church.

As they drove along, Gordon quietly mentioned what had happened in the car while waiting for her.

"I think it's an excellent idea," she said. "I can call about it tomorrow, unless you want to."

"Honey, do you want to be a landlord, be responsible for repairs and so on?" Gordon asked her.

"Sure," she replied. "It's no big deal. My father gained much of his wealth from rentals."

Gordon knew he was licked. It was two against one. He may as well join them he thought.

That Sunday, plans were made about the bay and to gear up for the new week. Gordon said he would call about the house for sale, and let his wife know. But first thing Monday, he was going to deliver that bay and her papers. He didn't want the mayor to visit again.

The next day, Gordon did call the reality company. The sale was listed at $35,000. Gordon asked if he could stop by that afternoon and inspect the property. It had rentals on each side, but only one side was vacant. The reality company would need to notify the renters that someone wanted to do an inspection. The secretary called back and said that Gordon could inspect the property at two. Gordon put in a call to his wife to meet him there at two. The Di Angelos met at the double at two, and the realtor handed them a speck sheet. They went into the empty side first.

The rental was well laid out, very organized. It could use some paint and updating, but for the most part, in good shape. The water heater was only two years old. The furnace was gas, and cleaned every year. The windows were also two years old and most likely replaced when the water heater was.

Then onto the rented side, which was being used by college kids. It was very cluttered, dirty, and not taken care of. Miranda shook her head. It wasn't going to be like this, if they had it. As it was, the college kids were so far behind on their rent which is why the building was for sale. They stood outside, and Gordon offered $32,000, as is, with the right and reserve to evict the current tenants. They headed back to the reality office to sign the paperwork. The broker there knew Gordon well. He sat down to advise them that it may be in their best interest to put their daughter on the title with them. She would be the primary owner. So that is how the deed was finalized. The Di Angelos became first-time landlords. And as it turned out, it was easy to find good tenants. The home needed little to no repairs, and it became a very lucrative deal for their family.

Gordon began to catch on to the benefits of renting. Yes, he would be paying the taxes and upkeep. Also, when they would get older, they could themselves occupy one of the homes in town to be closer to things. Or they would have a source of income. Yes, he liked this idea. Miranda was way ahead of him though. From time to time she would see a home, but Gordon was specific on what he would or wouldn't buy.

The Lake

SOON THE ARRANGEMENTS FOR THE birthday party at the lake were complete. It turned out they would all be staying for the weekend. Miranda bought April a new swimsuit, a one-piece that was yellow with tie straps at the back of her neck. It looked cute on her with her yellow curly hair. She packed more than enough clothes for the weekend trip.

Miranda made plans with Mrs. Marshall. It was agreed that Miranda should make fried chicken, Mrs. Marshall's husband loved it, and she herself wasn't good at making it. Also, there would be lots of food and treats. Some games were also planned, plus a hike, and swimming. A weekend full of fun.

April was ready and packed, but she was worried about leaving for the day. She and her dad had picked up twenty-eight ponies at two different auctions and some of them were fighting. Her daddy separated the fighters on opposite end stalls of the barn, and that ended that. His deputy, Bobby, agreed to give the ponies hay and feed the calves for them. Bobby had the day off and liked animals. Besides, they were paying him.

Soon they were in their car heading to the lake. It was early and it was slightly foggy. So they drove with the car headlights on. April felt sleepy with the humid air all around her. She tucked her pillow up under her head and closed her eyes. Her dad saw her and said, "Are you going to sleep?"

"I'm conserving energy," she replied, and he laughed at her.

She did sleep. The drive up to the lake was breathtaking. The trees were so green and beautiful. The scenes were awe inspiring, and Miranda and Gordon sat together just as they had when they were dating. Sometimes he would lean over and kiss her neck. April slept almost the entire two-hour drive to the lake. But she woke up just in time to see the entire span of the lake as they drove into the cove area.

It was a huge lake, the sight was breathtaking, and April was excited. They spotted the Marshall's truck. They had a picnic table all set up with some Tiki candles and a hot grill emitting smoke from something cooking inside.

Trevor ran to the Di Angelos, with his mother behind him. "Drive around to the left side. It will be closer to unload," she said. So they did.

Mr. Marshall came over to help unload the car, and he and Gordon shook hands. April noticed there was another boy there. He was much taller than Trevor and much quieter. Mrs. Marshall saw April looking at her other son. She came and took April by the hand taking her to the boy.

"April, I would like you to meet our oldest son, Hugh."

April said, "Hello."

Hugh answered, "Hello," back. Hugh Marshall was a tall boy with a round face and quick smile. His eyes gleamed with intelligence. They were the bluest eyes ever. He had ruddy brown hair and light skin. April couldn't help but stare at him, in a respectful way. Hugh Marshall was impressive even as a boy.

"So this is your birthday at the lake?" Hugh asked her.

"Yes, it is. I've never been here before, and it's very beautiful. I especially like the fir and evergreen trees."

Hugh was surprised. Not many girls paid attention to trees. They always liked the lake.

"Do you like hiking?" he asked her.

"Oh, I do. I like to take long walks," she said.

"And she likes raising calves," her dad said as he joined in.

Hugh's father was there and he complimented April on her fine work of raising calves. He had heard she had a large herd that she had hand raised.

"We too raise cattle," he said. "All Angus, purebred from foundation stock, just like my great-granddad did. They are hardy and strong cattle. We've been raising them for over five generations."

"Wow," April said. "I would love to see them sometime."

"And then you will," he said with a huge smile. "And then you surely will."

Soon the food was on the table, and everyone had a plate. April sat next to her dad, who was talking with Mr. Marshall. Trevor plopped right beside her, all smiles watching her all the time. April didn't mind it, but sometimes Trevor was a nuisance. He never stopped talking, and he made antics to impress everyone. He was an instigator for attention. April was having none of that today. She liked Trevor very much, but today, she wanted to let go. She wanted to experience the lake and the woods, and not worry about Trevor.

The women cleaned up the food. They packed it up in the back of the car on ice to stay cool, and also to ward off animals. As they lined up for the hike, April retied her sneakers and started out hand in hand with her mother. It was a nice walk all around the lake. There were side paths that skirted through the low ends. They saw deer, squirrels, a porcupine, some young foxes playing in the field, and in the distance a young black bear in search of some grubs inside a log.

The women chatted together, as did the men. And Trevor was

always in the lead, darting here and there. So Hugh and April walked together. Sometimes if the pathway was too narrow, Hugh would offer his hand to steady April.

As the two walked on they covered many topics. Hugh was quite friendly and could carry on a good conversation. Hugh quickly learned April was a worker when she outlined her daily "jobs." She didn't boast, but was more matter of fact. It was interesting to hear her ideas. She reminded him of himself. He learned she liked music. That she played the guitar and wanted to play the piano. He learned she liked sports—running, and all sorts of athletic things. And so did he. Yes, Hugh Marshall soon realized April was much more mature than he was—she was a serious individual. He enjoyed having her laugh at his jokes, and he loved to tell them.

Soon they were all back at the picnic spot. They ate some lunch, and headed down to the lake. The spot they chose was on their grandfather's side. He lived above on the hillside, but he could watch them down below. There was a free-floating dock for swimmers to swim to and climb on, giving them a rest if needed. It was common for people to swim, dock and swim again. The cove water was very deep, but you could see clear for quite some depth.

At one point, Mrs. Marshall suggested they take the stairs to see her father. They could take their bags up there, since they were staying with him. So after they dried off, they walked up the steps to Mr. O'Toole's home.

He greeted them at the door with such joy and laughter, "Come in. Come in," he said over and over. He embraced his daughter with a hug. Mr. O'Toole hugged both his grandsons, and acted surprised to see a girl. "Well. Well. Just look at what we have here," he said with a big smile.

He looked at Gordon and said, "You sure grow them pretty in your town." Gordon was proud of April and nodded for April to greet Mr. O'Toole. April stepped forward, looking the man directly in his eyes, and said, "I'm very glad to meet you, sir. I learned a lot about you from your grandson, Hugh."

"Oh, yes, Hugh. Hugh, my boy. Now that's one smart fella there. And he has an eye for pretty girls. Don't you, Hugh, my boy?" Hugh was embarrassed and said nothing. His grandfather came and hugged him, rubbing his head.

"All right now. What can we do? Something to eat?" he asked.

"Oh, no," came the replies.

"Well, let's go out on the veranda and watch the lake folks," he suggested.

The women went out on the veranda with Mr. O'Toole while the men put their suitcases in their appointed rooms. April was given a rollaway bed with the cutest Scottie dog on the coverlet.

Hugh, April, and Trevor went swimming again. The day was hot, and the cool water felt good on their skin. They swam around, then chased one another. Often April and Hugh sat on the free-floating dock talking. Soon Trevor left them to go back up to get something to eat. Hugh called after him to bring him and April something, but they both knew he wouldn't.

"It's real nice that you can be down here with us for the weekend. My grandpa really likes you. But then my Grandpa likes all the girls," Hugh said.

As they sat there on that floating dock, there was one set of eyes watching them, Grandpa's! He liked these two, a lot. Seeing his

Grandson interact with a young girl thrilled Grandpa. He had high hopes for Hugh. Hugh's father wanted Hugh to follow in his footsteps, to keep raising the Angus breed. But he knew his grandson could do anything he put his mind to. He was a leader, a follow-through sort of boy. He never complained about work, just got it done.

Yes. He knew Hugh could be anything he wanted. All he had to do was want it bad enough. And here was a little girl, whom he had learned much about from his daughter, a girl who carved out a life on her own, who made decisions that were down right good ones. And he liked that about her. Yes, he liked what he knew about this girl and what he was seeing now.

And did he feel the least bit guilty? Absolutely not!

It was almost dark as the two sat on that dock when the lights of the lake houses came on. It looked like little candles in the forest. April was looking skyward, answering Hugh, and all at once she felt her cheek wet. She did a double take, and realized Hugh had kissed her cheek.

As the two kids sat on the dock talking with hands in motion, in a flash, he saw his grandson, Hugh Marshall, lean over and kiss the girl. He couldn't believe his eyes!

On the floater, April couldn't believe it either. She wasn't stunned. She didn't jump into the water or run. It was a curious thing to April. It wasn't like when her mother or Dad kissed her, and it was only a kiss on the cheek, but it was nice. She didn't ask him why, but just let it go.

Yes, it was nice, It was given out of kindness and an expression of happiness.

To Hugh it was no big deal. He wanted to kiss her, and he did—nothing more. So no big deal was made out of the "kiss" incident. Life went on as usual.

The picnic was soon over. The Di Angelos and the Marshalls returned to Mr. O'Toole's home for the evening and a good night's rest. Mr. O'Toole was giddy with what he saw that Hugh did. It was very hard for him to keep it inside. One look at Hugh and Hugh knew there was nothing he could do or say. He only hoped his grandfather would keep it to himself. The kiss wasn't nearly as complicated as his grandfather was. Hugh avoided his grandpa at all cost, and went to bed with a book in hand without saying goodnight.

The next morning the Di Angelos left early. It wasn't yet daylight, but Mrs. Marshall could hear them leaving. She got up and saw a beautiful card left on the kitchen table for her father. She imagined it was a thank-you card for allowing them to stay and enjoy the lake.

Soon her father joined her in the kitchen wearing his brown robe. He picked up the card, read it, and handed it to his daughter. After reading it, he said, "They are nice folks."

Then he asked his daughter if they could come back for the Fourth of July. The summer would be in full swing, and he wanted her and her family as well as the Di Angelos to come back for the Fourth of July picnic. His daughter said she was sure it would be fine, but would have to talk to them. She hugged her father and said she had to go get dressed because the others needed to get up and be on their way.

As they went out the door, Mr. O'Toole took his daughter's hand and told her, "You take good care of my Hugh now. Won't you?"

It sounded so curious to her, so unnecessary, and she said, "Of course," and she left.

On the way home, her father's words came to her again. Mrs. Marshall didn't understand why he'd said it or the implications. But she knew in time all things would reveal themselves. So she pushed it out of her mind for another time.

The Talent Show

THAT SUMMER BUZZED BY. THE town did have the fair, and April insisted on being in the talent portion. She wanted to sing a song and play her guitar. It was a song she and her dad sang together. Both of them loved it and sang it often. The talent portion of the show was judged by the audience. They decided who would win first, second, or third place.

April chose "Ghost Riders" by the Outlaws. It is a story song about a cowboy who rights his wrongful ways. Miranda got April's costume ready. It was a flashy silver-white shirt with glitter, a white hat. She also bought fancy blue jeans with a big Concho buckle that helped hold her guitar at the right height. Miranda got her a new guitar strap and boots. April looked like show quality. She practiced and practiced and practiced that song to perfection without her dad's knowledge. April and her mom worked on the lines, cues, and body language until it was just right.

Gordon Di Angelo wanted to go to the fair. He always tried to squeeze in the talent portion, but often had to work. Now Miranda didn't like the fair at all, but for some reasonm she kept pressing for him to get off work to be there with her. All he could do is say he would try. And so that's what he did.

His deputies, Bobby and Ellis, also kept at him, saying they would cover the fair, and that it was only right that he spend the first fair with his family. Gordon thought they had bumped their heads. The overtime wasn't generous toward paying more for deputies, and Gordon *had* to work his shift. That's just how it was.

The day of the talent portion of the fair arrived. It was in the evening, but as luck would have it, Gordon had to work with one deputy. They had to walk the fairgrounds over and over. They had to respond to lost children, fights, people who had too much alcohol, stealing, locked keys in cars, accidents in the parking areas, stolen vehicles, assisting the ambulance, and crying children. It was all part of the job.

As the loudspeaker boomed, Bobby kept telling Gordon to go closer to that portion of the stage. Gordon thought, *Whatever!* and he did get a kick out of some of the contestants. There was an eighty-year-old woman who sang "Don't Fence Me In," and kids who just sang crazy songs. Some played fiddles, and some played guitars.

Gordon Di Angelo was just about to leave when he heard his daughter's name announced. He was astounded—he hadn't known. Bobby was soon at his side, carrying a small bouquet of flowers. Gordon was shaken. They'd kept this secret very well. Gordon stood on a side step of the bleacher to watch his daughter, and almost shed a tear out of pride.

April stepped to the front of the stage, and Mr. Donahue, who ran this event, asked her what she was going to do for her talent. "I'm going to sing a song that is my and my Dad's favorite song. We sing it together."

"Well, then," said Mr. Donahue, "Let's hear from April Di Angelo. All right boys?"

April looked at the band behind her and asked for the key. "One, and a two, and a …" and she began to strum her guitar, tap her foot, and sing.

A mean old cowboy went riding out one dark and windy day
Upon a ridge he did rest as he went along his hard way.
When all at once a big herd of red-eyed steers, he saw,
A plowin' through the raggen skies and up a cloudy draw.
Yippie I ay, Yippie I oh,
Ghost herd in the sky.
Their brands were still on fire and their hooves were made of steel,
Their horns were black and shiny and their hot breath he could feel,
A bolt of fear went through him as they thundered through the sky.
He saw the riders a coming hard, he heard their mournful cry.
Yippie I ay, Yippie I oh,
Ghost herd in the sky
Their faces gaunt, their eyes were blurred,
cowboys shirts all soaked with sweat.
They're riding hard to catch that herd, but they ain't caught 'em yet.
Cause they've got to ride forever in the range up in the sky.
On horses snorting fire, as they ride hard on you hear them cry.
Yippie I ay, Yippie I oh,
Ghost herd in the sky
The riders rode on by him, he heard one call his name,
If you want to save your lost soul from a riding on our range,
Then cowboy change your wicked ways
today or with us you will ride.
Trying' to catch the devil's heard forever across these
endless skies.
Yippie I ay, Yippie I oh,
Ghost herd in the sky,
Ghost herd in the sky,
Ghost herd in the sky!

April ended with a shaky, scary, spooky sounding "Ghost herd in the sky" on a high note.

She did really well, Gordon thought, and he waited for Mr. Donahue to come out.

"Well, folks. How did she do?" The crowd went wild. They hollered, whistled, and clapped. "Well, that puts you in the front of the board," Mr. Donahue said.

April stood on the sidelines, and soon all four deputies were at Gordon's side. Gordon laughed to himself because, in a way, April belonged to all of them too. They all loved her. And April was forever asking Miranda to make treats for them.

One last contestant, a twelve-year-old boy, played a fiddle, but not so well. You had to give him credit since he had only been playing three months.

Soon it was over, and all the contestants stood at the front of the stage. The crowd had to indicate who they wanted to win, and, my goodness, they chose April. Gordon was so proud he had tears in his eyes, and his deputies had wet eyes too. They shoved the flowers in his hand, and he was to go to the front of the stage to congratulate his daughter. As he picked his way through the crowd, his head barely cleared the stage. April came to him all smiles, saying, "I won, Dad. I won singing our song."

"I saw that, darling. You made your dad so proud. Look. I have tears in my eyes," he said, smiling.

"Oh, Daddy," she said as she leaned forward to leap into his arms.

It was a proud moment of his life. He held her like a lifeline. He loved his little girl so very much that his heart was bursting with pride. This moment he sealed in his mind and often recalled it when he needed her. She was his happy place in the world. As she grew, this moment was recalled time after time. It was a treasured moment.

"Hold on a minute, folks. It seems that Dad is here right now," Mr. Donahue said. "Come on up here, Pop."

Gordon waved his hand like "No. No. It's all right. You don't want me." But the crowd began to chant and cheer for Gordon to go up on the stage. Holding on to his daughter, he did.

"Now I understand this is your favorite song to sing with your daughter," Mr. Donahue said.

"Yes. Yes, it is," Gordon said.

"How about the two of you sing your song, just like you do at home? I think our crowd would love to hear their sheriff sing with his daughter," Mr. Donahue said.

Then the crowd cheered and whistled. Gordon looked at his daughter and asked her, "Do you want to sing this one more time with your Dad?" April winked at him and picked up her guitar. Someone handed Gordon *his* guitar, and he knew this had been a set up.

And who handed him his guitar? Why it was Miranda right there in the front of the crowd. She was all smiles. As Gordon was handed a chair, April stood beside him and they played just as if they were on the porch at home. It was easy, soft, and done beautifully. It was a moment in time Gordon Di Angelo and Miranda never forgot. It meshed his family together in public, a private moment shared with the community.

Gordon handed his daughter her flowers at the end of the song, and she hugged his neck. The crowd loved it, the show of love and affection of daughter to father and vice versa. It was so tender that for months this was talked about, and all agreed it couldn't have been better.

April did keep playing and learning songs on the guitar. She also began piano and violin lessons that summer, and loved playing. Music was a great part of the Di Angelo family, bringing much joy to others.

I Belong!

THE SUMMER BLAZED ON WITH so much to do. In May, Miranda made arrangements for them to go to her home in Mexico in August. But there was the entire summer to get through before that time. She bore down and pushed through showing her very best side to all situations. In July, the finalization for the adoption was scheduled for the third. It was the day before Independence Day, a most appropriate time.

There had been no notices of a lost child. No one reported her missing across the Midwest or into California. So when Missy called for them to come in at one for the finalization in the courtroom, Miranda was excited and nervous. She immediately called her husband at work. Gordon wrote the date on his desk calendar and circled it over and over while he spoke with his wife on the telephone.

"It's going to be all right. Don't be nervous. We have been together as a family for two years now, and it fits. I wouldn't want to lose her. Do you?"

"Oh no," she said. "I would rather die."

"I thought so," he replied. "Let's talk to April tonight. If you like, we can take the horses out for a ride and tell her." Miranda thought that was a most excellent idea. She used to ride a lot before she met Gordon, but life seemed to push her into another role. She could ride. He often encouraged her, but for some unknown reason, she was always busy. Miranda didn't make riding a priority, when in fact she loved to ride.

So that was that. Miranda would make a light supper of

sandwiches, go for a ride, and tell April the news. When April came home, she knew something was up. Miranda was evasive, and usually, she was straight-up forward. As Poppa came home, he hugged her and said, after supper, they were all going for a horseback ride. That thrilled April. She was excited that Momma was going too.

On the ride Gordon broke the news like this, "So, are you happy here with us?" he asked April.

"Are you unhappy with me?" she answered.

"No, but we wanted to ask you some questions to see how you felt," he said.

And with that April began to cry. She held her head down as Dobbins kept pace and couldn't look up. Miranda noticed this in an instant and reached for Dobbins reins and stopped. Miranda dismounted and held onto April.

"What's wrong, sweetie?" she asked her.

April looked up with tear-filled eyes and asked, "Did you change your mind?"

"Oh no, sweetheart. We didn't." Miranda knew intuitively how April was interpreting this conversation. "What Daddy is trying to say to you is that this week we have an appointment with our friend Judge Du Val to finalize your adoption and bond us as a family. We wanted you to have your opinion. That's all."

"I thought that we were a family. There's no going back for me. If you decide not to want me …," and she broke into sobs.

Gordon hopped off of his horse and picked her up. He held her in his arms and whispered, "Shhhh. It's all right. Don't cry."

Miranda rubbed her back and said, "April, you're so young. You'll find that men aren't as good at expressing their feelings as women are. They're different than us, and don't say things as we see them. They don't mean to be different—they just are. It's up to us to have eyes in our hearts to understand them. Now you know we love you. And we never, ever want you to leave us, but one day you will. One day you will grow up and want to leave. But for now, God has found you and brought you to us. We want more than anything in this world for the three of us to be a family, legally."

April looked at Miranda, and she understood. Her poppa was still holding onto her with tears in his eyes, saying, "I'm sorry, darling. So sorry. Will you forgive me for being such a dumb dad?"

April kissed his cheek and pulled Miranda closer to her. They all hugged and felt the healing power of love. Then her dad put April on Dobbins, and they all mounted looking at each other.

The three of them went to finish their ride. It was a great ride. They saw deer with their young. They saw a great horned owl flying across the meadow, a badger digging near the pines, a skunk family making their way to the creek, and many types of birds chatting away as they rode by. Yes, it was indeed a good ride to forget your present cares and experience the out of doors. They knew all would be well.

So on the third of July they all dressed in their good clothes and headed to their appointment. As they entered, the courthouse was fairly empty. They stood at the big chamber doors and then entered.

There was their good friend Judge Du Val. He got up and came down to where they stood. He greeted his friend Gordon with a firm handshake and a hug for Miranda. He then bent down and asked April, "Well, little lady, are you ready?"

April said, "I have been waiting all my life." He took her hand, and they went to the bench.

Judge Du Val rang for a court stenographer to record the event. He also had two witnesses present, Missy and one of the court sheriffs.

He then read a formal article, and then the court sheriff brought the papers to Gordon and Miranda. On the papers were yellow Post-Its to mark where they were to sign. Once signed, the sheriff put the papers back on the desk for the judge. Then the judge called April to come forward and sit in the witness chair.

"Now, April. Do you understand what we are doing here?"

"Yes, of course I do," she replied. "This is so they"—and she pointed to Gordon and Miranda—"will legally be my parents until the day I die."

"Well put," the judge said. "Are you in agreement with that?"

April looked at the judge, "Are you kidding me? Are you doubting me too?"

"No. No, I'm not. But I'm required by law to make sure there's no doubt in anyone involved. This is a very important and specific law that must carefully be handled in the right way."

"Oh, all right," April said. "I agree and never ever want to be away from them, not ever."

He signed the paper with two different pens, and then handed the papers to Missy to be filed in the courthouse. As Missy left, the judge came down from his bench and shook their hands.

Then he told April, "Now you are all a family—legally binding. No one can ever take you away. No one can tell you that you don't belong. The three of you are now a family, legally and forever." And they all cried happy tears.

"This is cause for a celebration," the judge said. Gordon told the judge they were renting a cabin up at the lake for the weekend. And he would love for him to come up and stay with them.

The judge's eyes lit up, and he said he would bring his boat if it was all right. So that's how they spent the Fourth of July weekend, her mom and dad, the judge and her, all having fun. There was swimming, hiking, playing music, playing games, and visiting with the Marshalls and Mr. O'Toole. Never again would Gordon be Gordon or Miranda just be Miranda. From that day forward, they would be Mom and Dad, Momma and Poppa. April decided that if these two were willing to take care of her, love her, and treat her like a daughter, then the very least she could do is show respect and call them Mom and Dad.

The Fourth of July came about so fast. The lake was awesome. There were hundreds of people there. Many stopped to talk. Some people would pop by and share a side dish of something and take a hot dog. It was like one huge, happy family. No one argued. No one was upset. They all had a good time at the lake.

April had such fun with Trevor and Hugh. They did everything together. They swam, ate, went on a boat ride with the judge who allowed Hugh and April to steer and honk the air horn. They both laughed and laughed. Yes, it was a special time. It was a time for kids to be kids, and adults to rekindle friendships of summertime friends.

That floater was still a hot spot for all swimmers who wanted a brief rest from swimming. Hugh and April sat on it as other swimmers would get on dripping the lake water all over them. The two of them just smiled and then laughed. They were like two water imps. They would race each other in the water and splash each other, developing a deep friendship. Throughout her lifetime, when calm was required, April would recall those summer nights at the lake—the stars in the sky, the twinkling of the lights, and the innocence of love.

My Mexican Family

THE MONTHS FLEW BY WITH horse shows, pony rides, and taking steers to market. Miranda was trying to pin down a time for them to take April to her home in Mexico. Her mother, Contessa, had called several times, but they had always been busy. School would be starting in September, and they had to go before that, so she made a note to speak to her husband when he got home that evening.

At dinnertime they had tacos and refried rice. *This is a good reminder*, thought Miranda. As they sat after finishing their meal, she brought up the suggestion of going home to Mexico.

Gordon inwardly groaned. He had promised and now he had to keep it. "Sure. You make the arrangements with your family—say about the middle of August—and we can go for a few days. I can't keep asking Bobby to take care of the calves and ponies, so try to keep the days to a minimum."

That stirred anger inside Miranda. She wouldn't consider the trip for only two days. She would find someone to take care of the ponies and calves. It was a lot to ask of Bobby the deputy, since he would have to work and take care of the animals. That wouldn't be acceptable.

Miranda felt confident she could find someone reliable to help them out, so she turned to church members. She asked neighboring friends who lived a half mile from them who were also members of their church to help out. They were an older couple who never farmed but liked animals. And with detailed instructions, they felt confident they could easily manage for two weeks, as long as the food was readily available for the animals and they were shown what to do.

Betty was Miranda's visiting teacher and her husband, John, was Gordon's home teacher. They were a lovely, spry couple who took their callings to heart. They were dependable and caring. They were the kind of people you couldn't help but love. They were going to stay in the Di Angelo home and bring their dog, Lucky, with them. It would be a vacation, of sorts, for them too. So now the three of them could go away and not have worry about the animals' care.

Mexico was going to be quite a trip. There was much packing, planning, and more packing. Miranda wanted to take many gifts to her family, not to impress them, but out of respect. Soon their car was loaded, and by loaded—the trunk and entire back seat were filled to the roof.

April sat between her parents on the front seat. Gordon said he felt like a huckster, and Miranda bristled. Gordon knew he couldn't reveal his feelings. He knew he had taken the most prized procession from the Fortonato family. Miranda was truly a gem, well-educated, and an honestly good woman. It truly had been God's plan for Gordon to have found her.

There he was, a returning soldier who had missed his bus. He was walking with a duffel bag over his shoulder when a kind man with a pickup truck offered him a ride. They were heading toward Mexico, and Gordon felt he could get a bus ticket there, then head for Fresno. But God had a plan.

The driver drove them to the Fortonato family ranch. They welcomed him in, he took one look at Miranda, and he was smitten. He couldn't reveal his feelings, but as he stood to pull out a chair for

Miranda to sit at the dinner table their arms touched. It was electric. They both felt it, and it was obvious by the look on their faces.

Yes, the Fortonato family wasn't thrilled a gringo took their lovely daughter away. But in time, both of Miranda's parents came to accept Gordon. He was a good man, a sheriff of the town, he stood for good and justice. He treated their daughter like a princess. Not all of the Mexican men in high standing were as good to their wives as Gordon Di Angelo was to their daughter.

When Gordon asked Miranda's father for his blessing, it was a very difficult thing for Manny. But he knew they would marry even without his blessing. And it was best to keep peace in the family. So within eight months of meeting a beautiful woman and being smitten, the two were married and promptly moved to Fresno.

They didn't see their daughter often. Manny suspected it was because of "their way"—family was first. Gordon was a proud man, he tried to fit in, but it just came hard for him. This had been discussed by Manny and his wife, Contessa, many, many times. Since this trip was planned, they knew something had changed, but they didn't know what it was. Their daughter never mentioned any changes. Everything was always fine, or they were busy. So with much anticipation, they planned to do all they could to welcome Gordon with open arms, love him, and show him he belonged.

As the miles lay behind them, Gordon put his arm over the back of his seat to touch his wife who looked at him and smiled. He knew she was a good daughter who loved her parents, brothers and sisters. It was never his intention to "take her away," but their life was in Fresno, not Mexico.

Miranda wouldn't travel without Gordon. Not even for a quick visit. Miranda felt they were life partners—where he went, she went.

It was the time of generations to "find" themselves, but Gordon and Miranda felt so lucky to have found one another. They complimented each other. They were soulmates and never would either go or do anything without the other.

By nightfall, they arrived. They were all tired, but the Fortonato household sprang alive with lights and movement. Many people came out to greet them and bring in what was in the car—trip after trip after trip.

"Miranda, did you bring us your whole house?" her mother asked her, laughing.

"No. There are many gifts for everyone," Miranda said.

Soon all of their things were brought into the house. The Fortonato famiy had been waiting to have dinner with the Di Angelos. When Contessa and Manny saw April, they were astounded and shocked. They asked their daughter what was going on.

Miranda Di Angelo took her husband's hand. They both stood behind April and said, "Mother, Father, this is our daughter, April. She came to us by God, and recently, we filled out the legal papers to have her become our daughter permanently."

Miranda's eyes were filling with tears. Both of her parents saw how much this meant to their daughter. Contessa stepped forward to hug Miranda and said, "We are so happy for you, for you both."

April stood still. She felt she had to wait to be recognized, out of respect.

"Welcome, little one. What is your name?" Contessa asked April.

"My name is April Di Angelo. It is a pleasure to meet you," and she curtsied. Mrs. Fortonato's eyebrows raised, and she laughed, hugging April into a big bear hug. "Come. Come sit at the big table. We have much to talk about."

And they all came—all twenty-eight of them. April had no idea a family could be this big. The room was immense. Huge archways led them into a great hall that was polished marble. And the table was made of inlaid trees, the leg, the top, the entire thing. It was a table of beauty, almost a shame to eat on it. The room was full of pictures of bulls, bullfighters, horses, and women in beautiful gowns with their hair done up and dripping in jewelry. On the wall was a stuffed animal, a boar with huge teeth. There were also spears on the wall, and to the left of the archway was the biggest saddle April had ever seen. There were tapestries hanging of hunting scenes and of beautiful birds. This could have been a museum, easily.

Manny stood raising his glass and using a fork to tap on it to make a bell sound. "Everyone. We are gathered here to welcome our daughter, Miranda, her good husband, Sheriff Gordon, and now their lovely daughter, April. Yes?" and he looked at April with a big smile.

They all raised their glasses and saluted the Di Angelo family. Then they all were eating and talking, and talking. Soon April felt sleepy and stood up. She noticed her mother and father were in a deep conversation, and they were unaware of her. April walked to the far end of the room and a woman coming through greeted her. It was Miranda's sister, Flora, and she said, "What do you want, Sweetheart?"

"I'm sleepy. I wish I could lie down and go to sleep. If that's all right?" April said.

"What beautiful manners. I need you to spend some time with my son," she said. "Yes. I'll take you to your room," and she did.

After a short while, Miranda and Gordon noticed April was

missing and inquired about her. That's when Flora told them she had already taken April up to her room for her to sleep.

"Yes. She goes to bed early, but she also gets up very early," said Miranda.

April slept a deep, peaceful sleep. In the morning, she got up early and walked to the kitchen. No one was there. She walked to the room where the meal had been. No one was there, but someone had cleaned that room from top to bottom. It was spotless.

April saw someone out on the veranda. It was Manny, Miranda's father. April pulled up a chair and sat beside him.

"What are you doing up little one?" he asked her.

"Oh, I get up early every day," she said. "I have chores to do, and I just wake up," she answered him.

Manny laughed. Most of the children here slept the day away, and it wasn't yet dawn. "What chores does a little girl do?" he asked.

April filled him in quite nicely, and Manny was astounded. He realized this girl wasn't kidding. She knew quite a lot about animals.

"Later today I would like you to meet the Monster," he said.

"The Monster?" asked April.

"Yes. He is like Diablo, the Devil. No one can touch him, no one. I bought him for my wife, and he has turned into the Devil."

April sat there enjoying the dawn. The sun hadn't come up yet, and it was foggy. She could hear a fox yip in the distance. She asked about it, and Manny said, "No, little one. That's no fox. It's a coyote. He's looking for his breakfast, and he won't find it here. Jose will shoot him if he comes even close."

April heard the rooster crow. She loved roosters. They had such personalities. April then began to hear the cattle and horses. The ranch hands were moving the cattle out. There were some dogs with the ranchers, Catahoula dogs, she was told. They were quite adept at moving the cattle. It was an amazing sight.

April was no longer sitting in her chair. She was leaning on the rail of the deck, watching every move.

"So, I hear you too raise cattle," Manny said to her. "Yes, I do. But they don't look like these," she answered. "I have Holsteins, Angus, white-faced Herefords, Charolais, and some crossbreeds. I would like to start a dairy, but Dad said no."

"Why did he say no?" Manny asked.

"He doesn't want me to have to do that every day, twice a day, and not be able to do anything else. But I think he's wrong. I think it is a job that I can do and make money. In time, I can employ others to do it, and I believe with all my heart, that dairies could end hunger in the world," she said.

"You do? How would that happen?" he asked her.

"Well, you see. When a cow goes down, whether from a heart attack, a broken leg, or for whatever the reason, that cow could be made into hamburger. One cow can easily make a thousand pounds of hamburger. Imagine all the people one cow could feed. If this meat was marked for the poor who wouldn't have to pay for it, then they would get their meat free. Not a cost passed onto the taxpayers. And if people wanted to pay for this good quality meat, they could buy it."

"I see you have pondered this in your mind before," Manny said.

"Yes. I have, and I know it can be done. One day I'm going to do that. I'm going to do my very best to end hunger in America," she said.

Manny was shocked and impressed. Someone so young to be so concerned is a very rare thing indeed. He knew his daughter wanted children, but what a blessing this little one was. She's so conscientious of the world around her, not just about her. He reached for her and hugged her.

"You call me Poppo. Okay? I'll be your Poppo."

Soon the household was up and about. They could hear chatter and dishes rattling. "I think if we don't go in soon, they will come out and get us." So they went back into the great room with the big table. Breakfast was awesome. There were thick slabs of thoroughly cooked bacon, hominy, grits, honey on freshly baked bread, eggs, pancakes, and ham.

April didn't eat as much as the others, but still she was full. She did take two apples with her and excused herself. April wandered down to the barns. In a short while, she was looking at a wooden round pen with a water trough and a hay rack that was full, but not touched. The building was large enough for three horses, but April knew there was only one in there. It was easy to guess who he was.

Diablo

He stood there in the dark looking at April, sizing her up. All you could see were his dark, glistening, beady eyes. He poked his head out. He was a black beauty with full mane and forelock almost hiding his eyes. He wasn't afraid. He had no reason to be. He was king here and he knew it. He was hoping for someone to make a mistake and let him out.

April knew instinctively all she had to know. She just watched him to make him a little uncomfortable and to see if she could get the stallion to pay attention to her. April sat there at the rail, singing songs quietly, and the stallion would shake his head and turn his rear end to her. April didn't care and kept singing and soon crunched an apple.

That got the stallion's attention. He turned and snorted, walking over as close to the rail as he could smelling for the apple. April bit off another piece and held it flat on her hand to see if the stallion would take it. The stallion squealed and ran away, dirt flying, to the far side of the round pen.

"Suit yourself," April said out loud to him. "It sure is delicious," and she crunched another piece. The stallion came slowly, curiously to see if he could get a chance for another piece. April again held out her hand flat with a small offering of apple on it. This time the stallion took it slowly and carefully, and walked away. Again, another piece and this time the stallion came and ate it, then stood there for more.

"Kind of nice having someone pay attention to you ain't it?" April said to him.

The stallion studied April. He hadn't encountered anyone or anything like her—a small thing who knew his mind.

"How would you like me to pet you and brush your beautiful hair?" April asked the stallion. Then he stood there motionless as April stood up slowly.

April put her hand through the rail and on the stallion's chest, then spoke to him softly. The stallion didn't move. April patted his chest and rubbed it while speaking softly, then running her hand along his side. The stallion looked but didn't move. April felt scars on his side and asked him, "Who did this to you?"

The stallion shook his head violently and April said, "I would never hurt you. This is wrong."

The stallion watched April. Although he wanted to bolt, he did not. This little thing was careful, had soft hands and a soft voice, and he liked it. Normally, people yelled at him, whipped him, and threw things at him. No one offered him a choice. This little thing touching him would take her hand away and ask, "Do you want more? Do you want me to stop?" and the stallion would move closer.

They began a friendship based on trust, and the stallion hadn't been this responsive in months. He put his great head close to April's head and smelled her. April put her head against the stallion's, and head to head, they stood there, feeling each other, testing each other, it was a meeting of souls. They both were lost in a sense of time. Both were searching for something, trust, faith, something. They stayed that way for a long time.

Then suddenly there was a calamity of noise, and the stallion backed away as workers pulled April away from the fence. April kicked at them and picked up stones to make them leave her. She didn't understand what they were saying in Spanish.

Mom came running along with her mother, Contessa, and other women. Poppo was in the back. "What? What happened?" they all asked.

One worker went into a tirade of words, his hands were flying, and April didn't understand one word. Momma and the women would look at her, and they made sucking noises of taking in their breath. April was perplexed as all get out. Poppo and Dad came up.

Dad asked her, "Are you all right?"

"Yes, Poppa. I am. I was meeting the stallion, and we were having a very nice visit when the men scared him and he ran away."

Poppo was there and said, "You have met the Devil. He is very dangerous, and you aren't safe around him at any time. Promise me you will never do this again."

April didn't want to promise. She saw something in the stallion no one saw or didn't want to see. She believed they were through with him and April had just begun.

"Okay. I promise I'll not sit here and give him apples ever again," she said.

Poppo calmed the women down and that was that. Dad on the other had suspected something different. He knew his stubborn, bullheaded daughter very well, especially when it came to horses.

Nothing more was said, and later that day, Dad asked if she would go for a ride with him. They took out the old jeep and he crossed the desert and showed her the creek beds and the wild animal areas. Gordon stopped and looked at her. Then he said, "Now I know how you feel about that stallion. I saw it on your face, but you have to respect what the Fortonatos asked of you. If you want to work with that stallion, I'm willing to help you, but you must have Manny's permission. You must."

"Dad, they are all afraid of him, and he's afraid of them. They haven't been so nice to him you know. He has scars," she said. "All I want to do is show him kindness and I know he will respond kindly back. He has a good heart. He has been hurt, ah, spiritually inside. You know? And I just want to help him to heal."

"I know you do. Oh, how I know you do," he said. "But you must have Manny's word first. Understand?"

"I understand," she said.

So that night April approached Manny as he sat outside on the steps. April knew she had to schmooze him. So she snuggled beside him on the steps and he asked her, "What are you doing, little one?"

"I want to ask you for a favor. One that you will not want to give me," she said.

"Oh. What is it?" he asked.

"First, you must be open-minded and know I'm not like anyone else here on your ranch. You know that, don't you?" April asked him.

"Yes. This I know," he said.

April looked him directly in the eye and said, "I want to heal Diablo. I know I can. I had success today, and I want to try, but I want your permission."

Manny was taken aback. "Diablo, no, no, no, no. I can't let you. He will kill you. You mistake him—he is not kind. He is finding your weakness, and when he has it, boom, you will be lying there dead."

"I don't believe that," April said. "If your workers hadn't come down, I would have done more with him."

"If my workers hadn't come down when they did, you may not be here with me now."

It was evident that Manny wouldn't give is approval. "I promise never to sit at that rail and feed him apples ever again," April said, and Manny was happy with that. However, there were other ways to visit the stallion without sitting at that rail, so April had to make other plans.

When everyone was asleep, April got up at 3:00 a.m. and went out to the stallion. April slipped in the side door near the inside rail by his stall. The stallion was aware she was there but hid in the shadows.

"Hello. I'm back to see you. I'm very sorry they frightened you, but I didn't and I'm here to reassure you we are friends," she told the black stallion. "I don't like the name they gave you. I'm going to call you Beauty, because you are so beautiful," she told him.

And with that the stallion came out of the shadows to smell her again. After a smell, his head went up and down as if in a greeting.

"Shhhh. It's all right, but you must be quiet so we can visit or they will not allow me here ever again. Do you understand?"

He bowed his head as if in submission and understanding. The two of them visited this way for five nights. On the sixth night, April felt brave and unlocked the gate to his stall. The stallion backed up, but that was all he did. He lowered his head and came toward April who stood very still.

The stallion smelled her, then put his great head onto April's chest and stayed there. Ever so slowly, ever so softly, April put her hand on the horse's jawbone and stroked him to his neck. The stallion closed his eyes and soaked in the kindness. Then he lifted his head.

April took a step toward the stallion and hugged his chest. Then she touched him all over, his legs, his withers, his sides, and walked around him, touching, patting, and talking soothingly to him. The stallion never moved. He stood there enjoying the kind attention.

For two more nights, this was their routine. On the ninth night in with the stallion, April stepped up on the rail and straddled his back. The stallion lifted his head and looked. He began to walk around in the round pen. April lay on his back a long time, talking to him, touching his neck, praising him.

Suddenly, the stallion stopped for there was a light shining on them both. It was Poppo, and he looked shocked. April talked to the stallion and the stallion turned to go into his stall. April slid off and out of the gate, locking it, and joined Poppo outside. The stallion came back out and followed her from the inside and stood at the rail.

Poppo just stood there, and then he said, "You disobeyed me."

"No. I did not. You forbade me to sit at the rail and feed him, and I didn't do that. Instead, I tamed him because all he wanted was love and to be accepted."

Poppo didn't know what to say, this little girl tamed the Devil. He had paid many trainers to come and work with this stallion and not one of them lasted or done any good. They all left angry and disgusted.

As he stood there reflecting on all the trainers, Poppo began to laugh, "Oh, my April. What am I going to do with you?" and he hugged her.

"You're not really mad at me are you, Poppo?" April asked.

"Sure, I am. See my face?" He was laughing. "We must keep this a secret. When you come out again to visit him, I want to come along and watch. Okay?" Poppo said.

"Sure, that's fine, but you may not make him nervous or frighten him. Okay?" April said.

"Okay," Poppo said. He took her hand and she followed him into the big house. "How about you and Poppo have a snack?" and he began to pull out meats, cheeses, and all sorts of food, cake and pies.

"Poppo, I would like a hot chocolate. If I may," April said.

"Oh sure, sure," he said, looking around. He didn't have a clue where things were in the kitchen. They had a cook and a maid, but they were asleep.

April looked around, and she found some in a cupboard. April ran hot water and put the hot chocolate in a cup, stirring it as she watched Poppo make a huge sandwich.

"You have some?" he asked.

"No. I'm fine with my hot chocolate, Poppo," April answered, but he still laid some cheese and bologna beside her.

Before too long, Contessa came down and was in the kitchen too. "What are you two up to?" she asked.

"We were hungry, eh, April?" Poppo teased.

"Yes. We got a little hungry." April winked at him.

"Oh, so we have wise guys here, sneaky, sneakers, with big secrets, eh?" Contessa teased back. She sat with them, and the two talked Spanish as April just listened to what she could catch.

Soon one by one the household was beginning to wake up, and a real breakfast was being prepared. April wasn't hungry, she was content. But most of that came from the pact that she and Poppo made about the stallion.

The day dragged on, and someone came up with the idea of having a big party before they left for Fresno. They would have a race, fireworks, lots of food, and games. April thought that sounded like fun, so she was all in.

Each night, April and Poppo would go to the stallion and each night more progress was made. By the time of her second to last day, April had a bridle on the stallion. April could easily rein him and stop him. The stallion responded beautifully.

Poppo was impressed. There was no doubt this young girl was a horse person, his kind of gal. He had hoped his son, Henry, would have been a horseman. He had great talent, but back in November of 1978, they'd lost their Henry in an accident. He was only twenty-three. Other than visiting his graveside on his birthday, no mention of Henry was made. It was too painful.

Poppo stood slapping his leg, "You must ride Diablo, uh, Beauty, in the race tomorrow. It would be a great surprise to Contessa, and the others. Henry Jr. expects to win on his gelding, but this stallion runs like the wind. I have seen him," Poppo said.

"I would race him if I had a saddle on him. You know that no one must know, and I'll have to be the one working with him," April said.

"Yes. I know that. Can you handle him? Can you manage it? I don't want you hurt in anyway," Poppo anxiously said.

"I'm sure I can, but I hope my dad is okay with all of this. Sometimes he is too protective," April told him.

"Your daddy loves you. He is so proud of you, and he has the right to know you are safe. I don't want Gordon upset with me either for allowing you to work with Diabo. I mean Beauty." Poppo said.

"When Dad knows how much good we did with this stallion, he will be glad. My dad loves horses and to make one better is always his goal. I know he will not be upset or angry," said April.

The next morning April was out early. She carefully saddled Beauty in an English saddle and bridle, then let him munch on hay. No one was allowed down near his area, no one.

Everyone was excited for the horse race. There were eight ponies. Henry on his gelding, Lightning, Paul was on a burro named Taco, and everyone hollered for April to go and get a horse. April said she would, and she asked her dad to go with her.

The Great Race

WHEN THEY GOT TO THE barn, April took her dad's hand and led him to the place that everyone was told to stay out. Gordon hesitated, but April pulled him along, saying it was all right. When Gordon realized what was going on, he was flabbergasted. He had no idea that April had been working with the Devil stallion.

"Don't call him that Dad. He really is a nice boy. His name is Beauty."

"Okay then. Beauty," he said to the stallion as he held his bridle, "you have precious cargo on you for this race. Be a good boy and bring my girl back safe," and he gave April a lift and out they came.

Some of the people screamed. Some ran away. April gave Beauty a little kick, and he trotted to the line. Contessa's jaw dropped, and all of the family and ranch hands were astounded. "How could this be?" they all asked.

The line of horses, ponies and burro were in place. One of the cousins held a hanky, shaking it out farther in the field. It was explained they were to race to the pole at the far end of the field, turn and come back across the line. The first finisher would win. Once the hanky dropped, it was the signal to start.

"Ready. On your mark. Get set. Go!" The hanky dropped. The gelding took off as did some of the ponies. The stallion was dancing nervously, and finally April gave him full rein, a small kick, and away he went.

April and the stallion had no trouble catching the gelding, but April took the turn wide. She chased Henry home, easily passing him long before that finish line and headed out to the desert. April laughed and laughed. This boy needed to run. He had been cooped up far too long. April didn't care if she was disqualified. This stallion was so much fun to ride, smooth in a run, and he needed to stretch his legs.

After about twenty minutes, the stallion slowed his pace. He snorted and began a prancing walk. April patted his neck telling him he was a good boy as they turned for home. They walked home so the stallion would cool out.

As they came up the dirt driveway, April could see many people waited for her and the stallion. When they got closer, she could see Contessa in the front waiting for answers. As April got close, she dismounted and stood in front of Contessa.

"I believe this is your horse. He is a Beauty, for sure, and that is his name. Respect him, treat him with love and kindness, and he will not disappoint you. I promise," and with that April handed the reins to Contessa.

Contessa was delighted. She had wanted this stallion against her husband's wishes. This stallion had been finely bred and was very expensive. Then he'd become useless, as no one could touch him. She wanted to know what happened, what made the change. But for right now, Contessa wanted to touch her boy. So she took him and walked with him away from the others.

Contessa began to tear up as she looked into the stallion's eyes and saw a void, a deep loneliness. "I'm sorry I have neglected you," she said to the stallion. "It was my responsibility to take care of you and I handed it to others. That will not ever happen again. I want us to ride like the wind, to go where we both can explore. I'll trust you and you will trust me, and your home will be my home. This I swear to you," and Contessa kissed her horse.

Then the stallion nickered to her. Never did Contessa ride another horse. Beauty would become even more beautiful with constant care and love from one owner. It was truly a happy ending for Beauty, as he found his forever home and someone to bond with.

Yes. Time after time, whether sitting at the table or after she went riding, Contessa and Poppo would talk about the time when April came and changed Diablo to Beauty. Neither one of them could think of a danger that existed where this little girl wasn't afraid, but eager and willing to take the risk for the sake of the animal.

April was known to have a true heart that beat for the sake of others. It was an honor for the Di Angelos and for their family to think of their daughter this way. April was special to them, a horse whisperer in her own right, and they wondered where this would take her.

The Di Angelos went home the day after the party. It wasn't sad, but the Fortonatos weren't happy to see them leave either. They found a greater respect for their son-in-law—he'd given their daughter a wonderful gift of this child. He too loved her. It was evident in everything Gordon did.

And for Poppo, he felt he had found an old soul, a kindred soul in April. Never in his lifetime had he met such a caring, happy young girl who willingly went out of her way for others. She was a real joy to have around, and he hoped to see much more of her.

They all hugged and hugged some more and soon they were in their car. It was more loaded than when they came and headed home for Fresno.

Hoping, Wishing, Praying

THEY HAD A WONDERFUL TIME, better than they could have imagined. But now they were all eager to get home to the animals—their own home, their own beds, pillows, and their normal routine of life.

That summer blazed by with April's rides, their church callings, and getting ready for wintering the calves. Her herd now swelled to over seventy-five calves. School was in full swing, and April was placed in fifth grade. April was now a year ahead of Trevor, but they were still good friends. April still practiced her guitar with her dad. It was a family thing they did.

She also took piano lessons on Thursday afternoons when she got home from school and violin on Fridays in school. April enjoyed her music teacher, Mr. Dobis. He was a patient man. Sometimes she didn't practice as much as she could have, and he knew it. But he would always say, "That was good, but let's try that again." He always used positive reinforcement for good practices. He was never so critical that a student wanted to quit. She never saw him angry or upset. Her mom would bring them a meal when they came for a lesson since they weren't wealthy. It was just Mr. Dobis and his wife, so it wasn't inconvenient to bring them a meal or something they enjoyed.

Another one of April's passions was that she loved to read, not fiction, but novels about history and facts. She was always learning about horse bloodlines. She knew all about Big Red, Secretariat, Seattle Slew, and others. She also knew who their parents were. She made it a practice to know about all the race horses that ran with a good record or who had won the Triple Crown. She just had an insatiable yearning to learn about them all.

April was excited to know that there could be a winner born who may never reach their potential. She would lay back on her bed and dream of owning a finely bred animal. Yes, she enjoyed daydreaming about owning a race horse with untapped potential. Not only did she dream about it, she prayed that one day she would have that chance—all she needed was a chance.

By late November the Di Angelos again found themselves looking for animal space. April had accumulated enough calves to fill three barns. There weren't only steers, but now there were young heifers. They had been picked up as sickly, but they had thrived under her care. They didn't want to keep the heifers in with the bull calves or steers, so they were again in search for another barn. The Kiefer family farm was available. Both Mr. Kiefer and his wife lived in the farm house, and they had a few cows. He still milked and sold the raw milk to a few customers.

Gordon and Miranda went one evening to visit them. They lived a mere five-minute ride by car on the hard road. Mr. Kiefer came out as did his wife, and they spoke with Gordon and Miranda about what they expected. They were in full support of having heifer calves there and offered to teach April all there was about milking.

Gordon wrinkled his nose. He had to interject that he wasn't interested in milking cows.

"You may not be," Mr. Kiefer said. "But what we hear about your daughter suggests just the opposite. We don't mind teaching her, and it is something a young person can do for an income," he said.

Gordon began to feel as if everyone knew what was best for April. And Gordon was struggling. He didn't want his daughter tied down like that.

Mr. Kiefer said, "You know, there are worse things a girl could be interested in. Sure, it would take up her time, but that would be less time for a young person to get into trouble. Our own daughter milked cows and went to college. She's now a registered nurse working in Knoxville."

For now, the Di Angelos wanted barn space and help to take care of the heifers. And the Kiefers were more than willing to do that. Their herd had decreased to ten cows, and it wouldn't hurt to add to their income. So it was agreed upon: there would be no rent required, but Gordon would be responsible for the hay and grain. He was allowed to farm the ground since Mr. Kiefer didn't feel up to doing it anymore. Gordon or whoever Gordon hired was welcome to use the Kiefer's equipment so long as they kept it in good working order.

As they drove home, they were satisfied, but in the back of their minds, they knew this was far from the end. April was always expanding, but never did she complain about the work, or that she was too tired.

The days flew by, and in late November, there was an ad posted in their local newspaper about an estate yard sale. The people had lived on the outskirts of Fresno for years. The husband passed away first. Then, when the mother's health began to fail, the daughter moved home to take care of her. The daughter was married to a man who was a wheeler dealer. Eddie was from New York. He had an eye for nice things, but he overextended himself many times. It was the daughter's parents who always bailed them out, and that had to stop. There would be no more help, the daughter explained to her husband. So the estate yard sale notice was posted in the local trade newspaper, and Miranda wanted to go.

She was interested in a few items and she knew that the couple had a house full. It would be fun to look around and pick up a few things that she could use. The sale was on a Saturday, so Miranda and April left early to head out for the yard sale. She took her car so they wouldn't buy big furniture. If she did, she knew Gordon would help her later that day when he got home.

When they arrived at the yard sale, there were a few people already looking at things lying in the driveway on benches. And some had entered the house. One of the women there knew Miranda from church.

Miranda asked, "Are there people still living in the house?"

"No," the woman answered her. "From what we know, the daughter left to go back to New York. It was too hard for her to stay since she missed her parents so much. The husband, Eddie, is in charge, and he has friends helping him with the yard sale. Everything here, lock, stock, and barrel is going to go, everything."

"It is funny they didn't opt for an auction with an auctioneer. They usually bring a much better price," Miranda said.

"Well, if you knew Eddie, he doesn't like parting with money. He likes making it," the woman said. "He felt he would lose too much with a live auction, paying for the auctioneer and runners."

Miranda shook her head. "Of course, he would have to pay the auctioneer, but the advertising was free. And as far as the runners, Eddie could have helped do that. Well, easy come, easy go," she said to herself.

April was at Miranda's side and asked if she could look around.

"Go," her mother said.

April walked to the down side of the property where there was a makeshift garage/barn. She noticed a tan mare in the pasture that had a bay colt. There was another gelding with them. He was a red sorrel color and very tall. She went into the shed, and it was very roomy. The floor was inlaid stone and the walls were old stone as well.

April saw an old steamer trunk in the corner and opened it up. Inside were documents and horse registration papers listing dam and sire. April's jaw hung open when she realized what she had in her hands. April was so excited her hands began to shake. She wanted to calm down and reread what she saw to be sure. She did, three times. Then she put the papers back into the trunk and ran to find her mother.

Miranda was in the house holding a gravy boat and a blue cobalt bowl. April pulled at her and asked her to come so she could talk to her. Miranda was a little annoyed and distracted. But she put her things down on a dresser and came to the side so April could speak to her.

April's eyes were wide and excited. Try as best she could, she could barely contain her excitement. She wanted her mother to understand exactly what she was saying. It was difficult at best. Twice, April explained what she had found

"Are you sure?" her mother asked her. "Yes. Yes. I'm positive. Please, Mom, buy that mare and colt. Please!"

Miranda walked casually out of the house, and there was a man standing there overseeing the crowd. "Excuse me. I was wondering what you knew about the horses there in the pasture," Miranda said.

"They're for sale," the man said, laughing.

"Oh, really?" Miranda said very casually. "What is the price for the mare and colt?"

"Ah, I think the mare is $350 and the colt $200," the man said.

"So that is $550 for the pair?" Miranda wanted to clarify.

"Yes. I believe that is right. I need to go and get a paper in the house to be sure."

"Okay. You go and do that because I'm interested," Miranda said.

The man went into the house, and Miranda followed him. She asked if she could use the telephone to see if she could get a trailer to haul the horses for her. The man said there was no hurry, and they could get them anytime during the week. Miranda knew better. Miranda knew that if indeed this was what April thought, then these two wouldn't be for sale for $550. She had to act right now.

Miranda called Gordon. She quickly explained that she needed someone to come out with a trailer as soon as possible. Right now, in fact.

Gordon hung up and called Mr. Kiefer. They were closest and did have a trailer and a truck. Gordon said it was needed right away and gave him the directions.

Excitedly, the Kiefers did come out within twenty minutes. He backed into the yard and stood by his pickup truck waiting.

Miranda, meanwhile, was in the house counting out as much cash as she had. She was short thirty-five dollars. She went outside and explained to the Kiefers, reassuring them that she could repay them as soon as she got home. Mr. Kiefer was glad to help out. He pulled out two twenty-dollar bills and handed them to Miranda. Miranda nearly ran to the house.

Meanwhile, April was in the barn lugging the steamer trunk outside. There was another man there who had thrown in brushes, lead lines and anything pertaining to the horses for April to have. He didn't know the Di Angelo family. To him, it was a kid buying trouble. The mare wasn't friendly, and the colt was nothing but trouble to him. Besides he had to feed them twice a day, and he wasn't fond of horses.

Miranda hollered for April to come to her, and she ran to her mother. "Now, April. I'm going to buy these horses for you, but you should sign the slip because they are going to be yours."

Miranda was a smart woman. She knew that April was a minor, and should there be any trouble, then it would be difficult to prove fraud because of April's age. So April signed the receipt for purchase. The slip was signed by the man as paid in full with the descriptions of the horses on the sales slip. Then he handed the slip to April.

The other man was now trying to catch the mare. April quickly ran to him and grabbed some grain that was in a bucket nearby. The mare heard that and came willingly. April snapped the lead rope onto her halter and the colt followed his mother playfully prancing after her. The mare stepped up into the stock trailer without any problem. As did her colt.

Once on, Mr. Kiefer tied the mare loosely in the trailer. Then he gave a wave, hopped into his pickup truck, and left, including the trunk and all of its contents. Miranda bought the two items she was interested in for change and got in the car. The two of them quickly caught up with the Kiefer's trailer, and they followed them to the Di Angelo's home.

Miranda was so nervous she felt like a criminal. But it was the responsibility of the sellers to know what they were selling. And she asked three times for him to clarify the price and item. He insisted he was right. The man did check the papers in the house, and the prices of the horses were exactly as he thought. So as much as she felt she did it right, she felt uneasy. She felt like there would surely be some kind of backlash over this.

She couldn't have been more right. The Kiefers pulled into the Di Angelo's driveway and waited. Miranda parked on the opposite side of the house. April got out and ran to the trailer to unload the mare and colt. Mr. Kiefer put the steamer trunk and other things in the barn for her. Miranda went in to give the money back to the Kiefers and to pay them for hauling on such short notice. She pulled out seventy-five dollars from the pony rides' money and brought the cash outside.

"Here, and thank you so very much," she said.

"Oh. This is a little much," Mr. Kiefer said, "No. No, it is not. You came right away when we asked and you loaned money to me that you didn't have to. So please take it with a note of gratitude from us."

He put his head down a bit and thanked her, then got in, and left.

April put the mare in the far end of the barn to give her some quiet time. This was a new home, and she would need to get adjusted. All horses were a bit nervous in a new home. The end of the barn was empty, as all of the ponies were in the lot. So the mare had a pen that was thirty feet wide and sixty feet long for her to walk around in and the colt to run.

April put a wafer of hay in the rack and made sure there was fresh water. She wasn't a mean mare. She only wanted attention. And that colt was just learning how to be good, and had a long, long way to go.

Miranda came out to the barn to see what her daughter had gotten her into. The mare had settled in quite nicely. She was munching on some hay, and the colt had April's utmost attention. She was handling him, touching his head, legs, and body. He was a curious, furry one with a spot of white on his forehead. The rest of him was light brown fur.

"Well, I hope this is what you wanted, April," she said as she watched her daughter.

"It is, Mom. You will see in time. This little guy has potential, and if we do it right, he will change our lives for the better," she answered her mother.

Oh, boy, thought Miranda, *here we go on another adventure.*"

But what she didn't know was April was spot on. The papers proved his lineage potential, and he had all he needed to be a winner. All he lacked was the skill and knowledge of a trainer. And, in time, that would come about in a most curious way.

Back at the estate sale, Eddie didn't come home until very late. He was thrilled with the amount of cash more than the checks. This way no one would know how much he had. The only trail would be the checks. He went to bed at 2:00 a.m. and didn't get up until 11:00 a.m. the next morning. He was walking around outside in the driveway and noticed one horse standing, the sorrel red gelding.

"Hey!" he hollered to his friend. "Where is the mare and colt?"

"Oh, they were sold," the friend said.

Eddie spit out the coffee in his mouth, "What?" he asked. "What did you say?"

"I told you they were sold," and the man brought the notebook out that listed asking prices of what was for sale.

Eddie was furious. "That's the price of the two statues of horses in the far bedroom, not real horses," Eddie said. "Who has them? Who bought them?"

The friend didn't know, as they were purchased with cash. "Great! Just great," Eddie said. "I paid over twenty-five thousand for that pair, and you sold them for $550.

"Holy God!" Eddie said, over and over. "We have to find out who has them. I have to get them back. Who has them? Who?"

"It was a kid. I don't know. I think her grandfather came with a trailer to pick them up," the friend said.

"Did you get the license number or the make of the vehicle, the color? What direction did they go?" Eddie questioned him.

"Look. I don't know. If it had been so damn important to you, you should have been here," the friend said. The friend was upset. He walked away, got into his sports car, and left. As he drove away, he was agitated. He'd willingly come out this week to help his friend. He'd taken a couple of unpaid days off from work, and this was the thanks he got.

Okay, so he lost twenty grand. Eddie has lost tons of money. It's not like he made a loan to buy the animals. Besides, all of the money from the estate is his anyway.

Eddie was guessing the worth as he always did, but he forgot to guess the value of a friend who dropped everything to run an estate sale for him. So far as the friend was concerned, Eddie could kiss his you-know-what. He was done! He was going home.

He circled the area, stopped at a quick shop for a bite to eat, filled his gas tank, drove back to Eddie's in-laws' home, got his stuff, and left.

Meanwhile Eddie was on the phone with the state police lying, saying the horses were stolen. The trooper said he would be out shortly, and by evening, he was.

The trooper was amused. He figured out quickly what had happened. He told Eddie, "You were paid for the animals. You admit that yourself. Yes, a mistake has happened, but it was your fault. You can't expect me to track down a person who paid the exact asking price for horses and then take them back," the officer said.

"Well, yes, I do. The price was for something else. The man who sold them didn't know," Eddie insisted.

"Well, it was your responsibility to have informed him," the officer said. "If you had other obligations, you should have had clear instructions for the people working at the sale for you."

The officer left and felt this wouldn't be the end of this. Eddie was pushy. He wanted things to suit him, not necessarily obey the law.

Back home, an hour's drive from the estate sale, Gordon Di Angelo came home to what would dictate his life for the next two years. The little colt was lively and had a big personality. The mare was sweet as pie. And Gordon knew these two were keepers.

He came into the house with April at the kitchen table pouring over the paperwork. He sat down beside her, and he too realized very quickly the treasure she had found.

"Is this real?" he asked her.

"Yes, it is, Dad. It's a dream come true. I have daydreamed, pondered, and wished for something like this to happen. To some this is just a lucky find, but to me it's a miracle," April said.

Yes, this was indeed a miracle. This little miracle would take April and her family so far that they didn't realize the precipice they were standing on. It was up to them if this would happen. Their hands were required to work hard, have dedication, responsibility, and grit for this little one to develop and realize his potential. For now, it was fun and games. This little one would have the best of life growing up as a race horse. And he would forever remember the kindness and love shown to him.

The pace of life was busy for the Di Angelos. That December, they were able to sell off more than half of all the steers for a huge profit. Gordon put the money away in a CD to be available should they need it. And he bought two more brick homes in town. He had no idea the cost of a trainer, but he knew, in time, they would need one.

April continued her chores. Every morning she fed the ponies and calves in the pasture. Then she went driving the four-wheeler to the Adam's farm and fed there. Next, on to the Earl James farm and fed there. She couldn't travel by road to feed the heifers at the Kiefer farm, but daily, her father checked in on them.

April's best job, the one she loved most of all, was imprinting the colt. The mother was unflappable and understood what April was doing with her baby. He was a naughty boy sometimes, biting and kicking. His mom would sometimes bite him. April was very adept at handling her baby, and she liked that it gave her some time alone.

Yes, April found her favorite thing to do. On weeknights when she had activity day and piano or violin lessons, she longed to be home with the colt. He was her boy, and April named him Native Son. That was her name for him, not his registered name. That would remain a secret until it was needed.

There was an Open Invitational Show being held at the sports arena complex for English riding, equitation, and pleasure classes. There were big money prizes, and, lucky for the Di Angelos, the classes were all day on Saturday. So Gordon picked up a brochure and entered his daughter in eight classes. Gordon knew that the flea mare would excel and be noticed.

When he got home, he discussed the show with his daughter. He said it was a good chance to be noticed. But April wasn't sure she wanted to be noticed. She liked her life as it was. On the day of the Open Invitational Show, the flea mare was loaded and the best equipment shined up ready for use. Miranda had made her daughter new riding clothing. They were bright yellow with flecks of red. Throughout the show, April's thoughts were elsewhere.

April knew many of the girls riding, but there were also many strangers in the competition as well. There was one woman she noticed who seemed somehow familiar, but she couldn't place where she knew her. So she dismissed that thought.

An older gentleman came up to her. It was old Mr. Artie who had been a real presence in the horse world for thirty years. He ended his career four years ago with his famous horse Roger. He was an avid breeder of beautiful show horses. He and Judge Du Val were good friends, and that is how April got to know him.

"How are you showing today?" he asked her.

"Very well," April said. "Flea By is a steady mare. She knows what I ask of her, and she willingly does it."

"Reminds me of my Roger," the man replied. Old Roger was an internationally famous jumping horse. "It is so nice to see you again."

"The pleasure is all mine," replied April with a big smile.

Roger had quit showing as a six-year-old. Now he was seven and retired for breeding, but he still had the magic. He was now a bit overweight, but he knew what he could do on a field of jumps.

Soon a woman was at Mr. Artie's side. "Hello, Daddy. Who is your talented friend?" she asked.

"Oh, that's April Di Angelo. She's riding the flea gray she calls Flea By," and Mr. Artie laughed. He loved the tenaciousness of this girl. She was young but managed seven-foot jumps with her mare better than most adults.

The woman came to April and asked if she could speak to her after the show.

"Sure," April said. "I don't mean to be rude, but I must go. I'm third up," and she reined her horse to the entry area.

Artie and the woman stood there watching the jumpers. "I like her style," the woman said. "She's gutsy, has poise, and is a talented rider. I would like for her to come and ride with us," the woman said.

"You can't be serious," her father said. "She's still very young."

"That works," the woman said. "And I like to keep every option open."

As it turned out, this was Maria, the woman in Maryland who watched April ride with Barbara. Maria was a talent scout for the US Olympic Team. Recently, the team had suffered a loss. One of the women riders had fallen and broken her leg, and they couldn't find an alternate rider. She fully intended to ask this young girl to ride in her stead. She wasn't a good rider. She was great and managed her pony over seven-and-eight-foot fences with ease and confidence. The problem was they would need a horse, and that is where her father came in.

"Dad. What are the chances of getting Rodger into shape for the US competition?" she asked him.

Her father looked at her and saw she was quite serious. "He can be ready in four months with careful planning and training," he said.

"Well. Get on it, Dad. Linda fell and broke her leg. She's out, and I'm going to ask the parents of this girl if she would be allowed to ride in Linda's place."

He showed her the Di Angelo's spot. Both of her parents were at the competition, but she would most likely find the dad at the rail watching his daughter.

That's exactly where Maria found Gordon Di Angelo. He wasn't only watching his daughter, but he was riding with her in spirit. She stepped in closer to him.

"She's a great little rider," she said.

Gordon looked to his left and saw the woman. "Yes. Yes, she is," he agreed. "And you are?"

"Maria. I'm Maria, Artie's daughter, and I'm a talent scout for the US Olympic Jumping/Equestrian Team. I would like to discuss with you the opportunity that your daughter may have if she, and you as her parents, are interested," she said.

"And that would be?" Gordon eyed her closely.

"That would be for her to ride this year for the US Olympic Team *if* she made the cut. You see, we lost one of our experienced riders and have little time to find another. I believe your daughter may have the guts and tenacity to handle riding for the US Team."

"Whoa, there," Gordon said. "Our daughter is still very young, and she has a lot on her plate."

"So you're saying you aren't interested?" Maria asked him.

"I'm saying that I would love to discuss this with my wife and daughter before I make any decision whether to say yes or no," Gordon replied.

"Great! Here's my card. I'll be in town for two days. If I don't hear from you, I'll know you aren't interested." And Maria handed Gordon her business card.

"Number 138. Number 138. You are up," was the announcement, and April entered the ring with Flea By. She took the mare around one pass and then began her jumping run. There were eighteen jumps to be memorized in the jumping pattern. The horse was to respond to the rider, not too fast, not too slow, and clear all of the jumps without a fault.

April was already into jump four when she was looking over her left shoulder at what was coming. She leaned into Flea By to give her some speed for the eight-foot jump.

Maria liked her riding skills. She anticipated and looked for her horse. Not all young riders had this presence of mind. As April and Flea By went over the waterfall, there was complete silence. So far no one had cleared the bridge jump, but there wasn't one sound. Only hooves in a run and then nothing but a soft landing. They had easily cleared the eight-foot bridge jump and water.

Gordon was clapping as were many of the spectators. Only two more small jumps and April and Flea By's run would be over. They did it with not one fault, and she made a pass going past her dad.

She was smiling from ear to ear and slapped his hand as she went past. Maria liked the bond these two had. She knew, if they said yes, April would have the support she needed.

April exited the ring with help from a valet who congratulated her. "Thanks so much," April said. She knew it was important to be kind to everyone. They make the effort to compliment you, so say, "Thank you."

April dismounted and brought Flea By to her dad near the rail. Maria was just leaving. She congratulated April and patted Flea By on her neck, and then she was gone.

"Who was that?" April asked.

"That was a talent scout for the US Olympic Equestrian Team, and she's interested in you," Dad said.

"In me?" April laughed.

Then suddenly before anymore could be said, the judge was in the center of the ring with a microphone calling riders into the ring. The results of the day were in. April's number 138 was one of the numbers to reenter the ring.

Maria was on her way out, paused at the bleachers, and went up five steps so she could see the field of riders better.

All of the riders were mounted and sat in a line. The judge began announcing the winners from fifth place to first. As he called their number, the rider would rein his or her horse to the front, pick up their ribbon, plate or pin, then leave the ring.

Maria was betting on April winning grand champion. She had been flawless in all eight of her competitive rides. She was always in first. Finally, number 138 was called, and indeed April had won the grand champion of the day. She urged Flea By forward to get her ribbons, plate, and pin.

The judge asked why she picked such an awful name for such a beautiful pony. April told him it was her name before she got her, and since the pony responded to it, there was no sense in changing it.

"A name doesn't make you what you are," she said to the judge. The judge smiled and agreed with her.

April exited the gate for the last time. She saw Maria wave to her with both hands in the air clasped together to congratulate her. It was nice of Maria to do that, but April didn't know who she was. But in reality, she did, and soon April would remember.

Her mom and dad were there and helped her untack Flea By and get their things packed up to leave for home.

"Boy! What a day, kiddo. You cleaned house."

April smiled humbly at her dad. She was tired. It took a lot of memory, patience, and endurance. It was stressful in competitions, but she and Flea By pulled it off together. She missed the bay. She was the other go to mare that always pulled her weight and never disappointed. Flea By wasn't as flashy as the bay, but every bit as good, dependable, and productive in a show as the bay.

The ride home was dark and quiet until Dad spoke up.

"You will never guess who spoke to me today, Honey," he said to his wife.

"Who? Who did you talk to?" she asked. "Remember Artie? He was an Olympic rider with that big heavy-looking horse, Roger, who won time after time in the Olympics? Well, Artie was here, and so was his daughter. She's a talent scout for the US Olympic Equestrian Team. Maria wants us to call her to have April ride this year for them. It seems one of their most experienced riders fell and fractured her leg, so she's out," Gordon told her.

"Really? She wants to have our April?" Miranda asked. "Well, she wants April to try out to see if she can make the team. She believes she will, but April needs to try out first," Gordon said.

"Where does this happen and when?" Maria asked. She was interested in the details.

"I have her card, and she wanted us to call her within two days. If we don't call, then she'll know we, and April, aren't interested."

The Olympics? April was listening closely and wondered what her parents would like her to do. She was interested, but she had chores to do and couldn't travel long distances.

Her mom looked at her over the seat. "Would you like to try out, April?" she asked her daughter. "You never know. You might be just what they need, and you would be representing the USA you know."

April sat there wondering about all that would be required of her. She knew she wouldn't be staying at home. She knew she most likely would be away for maybe months, and she didn't want that.

Her mother saw the concern on her face and said, "Don't think yourself out of an opportunity. I'll call and see if we can work it out. If you want to do this, we'll make sure it will be done. Okay?" and April touched her mother's arm and smiled at her.

Maria fretted. She looked at the telephone each time she came into the kitchen. She checked the answering machine, no messages. She was hoping *they* would call, but nothing yet. On Monday at eight o'clock in the morning, Maria was coming down the hallway steps when the telephone began to ring. She half ran, half jumped down the stairs, to get to the phone. She tried to calm herself and *sound normal.*

"Hello. This is Maria."

"Hello, Maria. This is Mrs. Di Angelo. You gave my husband a card at the horse show this past weekend. You asked that our daughter come and try out for the team. I'm calling to say we are interested."

"Oh, you are?" Maria tried to sound calm and uninterested. "Ah. I know this is short notice, but is there any way that you could come over so we could discuss what is needed?"

"How about today?" Miranda asked.

"Well. Today or tomorrow, but it can't be any later than Wednesday," Maria answered.

"Okay," Miranda said. "How about tomorrow? I can ask my husband to come, and April will be there too."

"Oh, you both must come to sign papers, and, yes, April should come as well," Maria said.

"You must understand. My husband is the sheriff of this community and can't just take off of work. It has to be approved or have someone cover his shift," Miranda said.

Maria did understand, but it was required that both parents come if a minor was involved. And she explained that to Miranda.

"Let me call my husband and I'll call you right back," Miranda said.

She called her husband, who was in the squad car, and explained what was required of them.

"Okay," Gordon said. "I can take off tomorrow and work on Saturday. I'm sure Adam will appreciate a Saturday off. Go ahead and make the meeting for tomorrow. And remember to call the school. They should allow April the day off for educational reasons," he said.

So the appointment was set for the next day. They went, they sat, they learned, and they signed the bottom of the paper. Next April signed on the line. Then they wanted April to leave in a week, to join the team for training. Just like that!

As they drove home, they began realizing what they had just agreed on.

"I can get up a little earlier and feed the ponies and calves. I can also stop at Mrs. Adam's farm on the way to work," Gordon said.

"Nonsense. I can feed the animals at home and take the four-wheeler out to the Adam's. It would be a nice change for me. I'll learn to appreciate what my daughter has been doing every day. I don't need to be out there at the crack of day, and it will help fill my day."

"Okay. Yes, that makes more sense to me," Gordon said.

April sat there mulling it all over in her mind, then she said out loud, "I'm not going. I'm not changing my life so much that it makes everything hard for everyone else and easy for them. They are the ones looking for help."

Her dad thought about what she said and agreed with her. "You know, Miranda, she's right. If they really want April, they would be willing to make some concessions. There are many riding facilities around here, and Artie lives here with his horse."

So the next day Miranda was elected to give Maria the news. Maria answered the phone, "Hello, this is Maria."

"Hello, Maria. This is Miranda Di Angelo. I hope this call finds you well," Miranda said.

"It does," said Maria.

"Well, I have news for you. Our daughter is not willing to up and leave. She has many jobs to do here on our farm. She gives pony rides and raises cattle, and she's not willing to leave. So you're free to tear up our contract and find another rider."

"Hold on a minute," Maria said. "You signed a contract agreeing." Maria felt panic stricken.

"We signed as April's guardians, and April also signed. She's ten years old, so April said for you to sue her."

"Now wait a minute. I'm at the end of my rope," Maria said.

"We know that," said Miranda.

"I like your daughter," said Maria.

"And we love her," said Miranda.

"She rides like the wind, and we need her," said Maria.

"Then find a way for her to stay home and train for you," said Miranda.

And then Artie's name came up, as his horse needed conditioning, and that was the horse April was to ride. Maria knew the team needed her, and she knew her dad's facility would work nicely for April and her family. So that's how it was to be.

If the riding team was concerned, they were welcome to come and see her for themselves. So that was that. Every day after pony rides, April would go to Artie's stables and train with Old Roger. He wasn't old. It was his name. They did jumps, riding, and conditioning, over and over. After four months, both of them were ready. April's butt was hard as a rock. She and Roger made an excellent team. He was mindful of her in every way, and she anticipated everything about him. They rode as one. Her birthday party was held at the stable, and Flea By gave rides.

One weekday evening, some of the team members came to watch April ride. Tully was irritated that the newest member, who was the youngest, wasn't willing to join them at their training facility in Florida. Once he met her, he understood.

Here was this pint-sized girl, who needed a lift to get on Old Roger.

She rode fearlessly over eleven- and twelve-foot jumps, encouraging Roger, who was the seasoned one. Yes, she was something else. She was adaptive, responsive, alert, and ready for whatever came her way. To say he was impressed was an understatement.

After four passes, the trainer and April were aware there were several people in the training building with them. Tully walked up to the trainer while a woman with short, dark hair came over to April. April hiked her right leg over the saddle and slid off Roger.

The woman walked up to April to start a conversation when April extended her arm to shake the woman's hand.

"Hello. I'm April, and this is Old Roger. It's a pleasure to meet you. I'm sorry, but I didn't catch your name." That was because the woman hadn't said who she was.

"Oh, excuse me. I'm sorry," the woman said. "My name is Elaina, and it's my pleasure to meet you. I'm on the US Team, and have been so anxious to meet our new team member that I just had to come. I hope you don't mind."

"No. I'm glad you came. For some time now, I've been doubtful there was a team. I hoped there was. I thought about it a lot, and now I know you're all real," April replied.

The woman laughed. "Yes. We get all serious and caught up in our training that days and weeks fly by. But we knew we just had to come and see your progress. I must say, your riding impressed me and Tully as well. Tully is my husband and Captain of our team.

The two of them with Old Roger walked over to the trainer, who was discussing the levels of training April had completed and what was left to do. The four of them stood there when Old Roger snorted for attention. They all said, "Awk," for Old Roger blew his nose on them.

"You still like to be the center of attention. Don't you, old boy?" Tully patted the horse on his neck. "I hear you're almost ready. And, as much as you don't want to join our team in Florida, I was wondering if we could get you to come to Virginia two weeks before competition. That way we could all get used to being with each other and our horses to get the jitters out," Tully said to April.

April dug the dirt with her toe. She was comfortable in her setting. She was close to home, and could get all her chores done. Quite frankly, she was busting her you-know-what with this training. She also understood the importance of being with a group, the comradery of others for support and suggestions for improvement. April looked at Tully with the maturity of a much older person frankly stating her thoughts. April said she would need to speak to her parents, but felt that Tully was right. He wasn't asking too much. But April didn't want her work to fall onto her parents who did so much for her already.

Tully was amazed. He and his wife, Elaina, didn't have children. Their demands in showing kept them keenly aware that children would have to wait. He was impressed by April's maturity and her blunt honesty. She wasn't rude, but stated her thoughts and well, for the most part. Tully often dealt with adults who acted like they were ten.

"My dad will come by to pick me up," April said. "Why don't the both of you come out to our farm? You are welcome to stay and have dinner with us. My mom would be upset if you did otherwise. I'm sure she wants to meet you both and speak to you, and you may as well stay overnight. Our attic is finished nicely with a big bed. It has privacy, but you'd have to share the upstairs bathroom with us," April said.

Tully and Elaina thought about it while April finished her lesson. They decided that they may as well, this way arrangements could be made for April to go with them in order to be ready for the competition.

When Gordon Di Angelo came to pick up his daughter from her riding lesson, he met Tully and Elaina. He called home to give Miranda a heads-up, to let her know what was coming. Miranda threw in a meal she had frozen a week before, a large beef roast with potatoes, carrots, rutabagas, celery, and spices. It had been precooked and would need to thaw and simmer in the oven. She pulled out some of her frozen, homemade wheat rolls as well. She practically ran with Ruby at her legs to the attic to make sure it was straightened up and clean. Then she opened a window to freshen up the room, and put out a box of tissues.

They arrived within twenty minutes. Gordon with April and the couple pulling a big trailer. Miranda feared change was coming, and in the back of her mind she knew it would. She knew that this was meant to be somehow from the beginning when her husband told her about meeting Maria those many months ago.

"You have to accept this Miranda," she said to herself. "She's not yours. She's a loan from God who generously gave her for you to care for."

Miranda knew this, and, as hard as it was for her, she knew this was the first step of April leaving them. She knew there would be many more steps to come. They all piled into the house. April slipped upstairs to shower, so she was clean for dinner. Ruby kept her vigil at the bathroom door while Gordon showed the couple to the attic. They were impressed with how roomy the attic was, comfortable and quiet. Soon they were all downstairs and April finished helping

Miranda set the table. As she finished, she put her arms around her mother's waist to hug her.

Miranda stopped rushing, put her spoon down, and embraced her daughter. She kissed her forehead and squeezed her tight. "I love you, April. I'm so blessed, you know?"

April couldn't answer. She felt that old familiar lump in her throat that kept words from coming out. It was April who felt gratitude. She knew what being left behind was. Gordon and Miranda changed their entire world to take care of her. And, now again, she was dumping on them.

There was a flurry of talking at the dinner table. Tully explained that April should be with them at the very least two weeks before competition, but a month was best.

Gordon looked at his wife and said, "We can arrange that."

April had to excuse herself from the table. She had homework to do.

After April left to go do her homework, Tully said that he didn't want to unnecessarily burden them with more work. He fully understood from April about her chores and that they would fall on her parents. That's what was bothering her most. Miranda knew. She knew that her daughter bore a lot of responsibility, but two months would teach her and her husband all that her daughter did. April was never selfish in the reasons of wanting calves, they all benefited from her work.

"We can manage," said Miranda. "Between us and some of our friends, we'll get it all done. We would be proud of our daughter to ride in the Olympics and represent our country."

Tully slapped his thigh and said, "That's the spirit. She'll be gone and back in no time. When you see her on television and her accomplishments, that's when it will all be worth it," he said.

Gordon Di Angelo interrupted Tully and said, "She has always been worth it," and then he explained briefly how April came to be with them. "I just want her to be safe and cared for. She's not a baby, but she's so young. I get concerned that she's so far from us."

Tully and Elaina understood. They had lost many riders over the years due to family conflicts.

Two months was all they were asking for, two weeks in Virginia, and then to Germany. Next Gordon shook Tully's hand and said, "We are grateful for this opportunity for our daughter and we are willing to do whatever it takes to help you as a team achieve your goals."

"Well, there's a problem with money as well," Tully said. "We aren't financed heavily and any contributions you can make would be appreciated. The cost for your daughter, her transportation, from start to finish will be about seven thousand dollars."

Gordon and Miranda looked at each other. The commitment was huge, but they were all in. If they had to take a loan, they would.

Gordon said he could give them one thousand dollars right now. And in a few days, he would send them a check to their address, and it would be there before they were. Tully and Elaina thanked them both. They knew all too well what a hardship this was going to be on them.

As they lay in bed, Gordon and Miranda couldn't sleep. She snuggled close to her husband, and he put his arm around her.

"Where is our little girl going?" she asked. "She's going to take us on an adventure, a once-in-a-lifetime adventure. There is going to be so much pressure on those little shoulders, that I …," but he couldn't finish his sentence. They both laid there thinking, not for themselves, but for her.

Then Miranda said, "So this is parenthood?"

Gordon replied, "No kidding." And they both laughed.

The next morning, everyone was up early except for Tully and Elaina. All chores were done. Miranda wanted to show Gordon that if they sold five to seven steers that week, it should easily cover the cost for April. Gordon agreed.

Miranda also said she was going to ask for help at the farm. Before April had started training, and they thought she might have to leave months ago, several church members offered to help. Now it was only two months, and Miranda was sure they would still be willing to help.

And that is how it was. There were four families who threw in their support for the Di Angelos. The husbands alternated coming out with their teenage children to feed animals and help when it was needed. Often Gordon filled their gas tank because they refused money. It sure took a lot of stress off the town sheriff, as there had a lot of criminal activity during that time.

Gordon Di Angelo didn't sell five or seven steers. He sold ten of them, sending a check for twenty-five thousand dollars to the address Tully and Elaina provided. He wanted to be sure to leave no doubt they were doing their share. They were totally committed to the team.

April packed her things with help from Miranda and Elaina. Elaina assured them her laundry would be done as needed, but she didn't need a lot of things. What was most important was her riding gear. April would need to dress like the team. Her clothing would need to be ordered soon in order to be ready in time for the competition. April needed to talk to her mother, so when Elaina excused herself to go to the bathroom, April closed her bedroom door.

April took her mother's hands and put them around her. "This is what I'm going to miss most," she said. They both began to cry.

"We love you, April. You know that. You know your dad and I would walk around the earth for you." She kissed her daughter's cheeks and forehead.

"I can't call you, and I know you can't be there. I must steel my heart to be hard and not think of you, or this will happen." April pointed to her eyes that were dripping tears.

Then there was a knock at the door, "May I come in?"

It was Elaina. "I understand how the two of you feel, and it's normal. We don't get to see normal too often," she said. "There are so many families who don't have support. April, I want you to know how lucky you really are. You have two parents who love you and who help you. You know that after this is all done and over with that you are coming home—home to them. And hopefully, there will be some kind of medal around your neck, and that will depend on you. Yes, your parents will miss you, but they have a lot more to do to keep them busy. As do you. You will be learning. Both of you can think about each other, and what you are sacrificing to achieve your goals. And then, before you know it, this will all be over."

"She's right, you know," Miranda said, hugging her daughter. "You are a strong girl, in here." She touched April's chest. "We can do this."

She let her daughter hold on for as long as she wanted to. Then they all headed downstairs to say goodbye and head out. Old Roger was going to follow them with his handler later that morning.

Gordon was determined not to show tears. He needed to be strong for his daughter. He kissed her cheek and her head. Then he hugged her and turned her toward Elaina, who quickly put April in the back seat of their truck. Gordon lifted April's suitcase up into the bed. He knocked on the dark window at his daughter who was beginning to cry.

"It's all right, darling. We'll be waiting and watching, and will see you soon."

Gordon had to turn away. He just had to. He stood with his wife on the driveway as the truck backed out and drove away. Then the two of them held onto each other. This was hard. Miranda's tears soaked into his shirt, and some of his tears mingled with hers.

Yes, this was parenthood. Doing all you can for your child to succeed. Not giving them everything, but teaching them. Teaching them to work and to achieve merits on their own by their own two hands.

Speaking of hands, Gordon hoped that April took her medication with her since they left so quickly. He asked his wife, who wasn't sure, so the both of them went back in the house to check.

We're Really Here!

THE MONTHS FLEW BY. THERE wasn't a day the Di Angelos didn't think of their daughter a thousand times, and it was the same for April.

She met the team of eleven riders. As they practiced, it was determined that April was third rider. Third out of eleven wasn't so bad for a ten-year-old. The truth was anything can happen, a fall, an injury to a rider or horse. Tully had to keep his options open.

They flew to Germany two weeks before the Olympics. Elaina kept April with her. There were many, many competitors in many different events. Elaina felt it was best if they stayed apart from them until after they finished their event, to keep the jitters down.

The day of the competition, the heat swelled, the air was sticky, and the horses were restless. The grounds were wet when they reached the barn. April walked to Old Roger with a carrot. She scratched his ears fondly while he held his big head to her. These two had bonded. Old Roger would look for her, whinny to her when he would see her coming, and that was a good thing.

The day of the show, and after the horses were all tacked up, they walked their horses to the show arena. The first event was an outdoor, timed event. It consisted of racing down a hill, crossing the timed barrier, and completing a series of jumps without fault and under the lowest time.

After their competition, the United States was in second place behind Germany. That earned the riders a bronze medal. Old Roger and April breezed through their competition and won so easily that there were complaints to check her age. That took several hours for the paperwork to be found.

It was very unsportsmanlike to behave that way, April thought. And for that, she was determined to do even better. They were all there to win. There was no reason to pick on her. Now they were going to be sorry. She didn't practice all these months, travel to Germany, and put a burden on her parents, to lose. No sir. She came to win.

The indoor competition was complex and total concentration was needed. The bleachers were full of spectators. Some were family members, and some were just fans. April imagined her parents were there, somewhere. It helped her to cope.

It seemed like it took forever until the United States had their chance to compete. Elaina was concerned about how difficult the course was. She spoke to April, who said she memorized it on her hand, using her knuckles and fingers to know the pattern. Elaina thought it was clever of her.

And then it happened, the unexpected. One of their riders came at a jump hard when a spectator popped a bag. It frightened the horse, which turned and bolted, knocking his rider to the ground and dragging him. The rider was disoriented and confused. The spectator was a bad sport, who was against the United States. He was immediately thrown out by the police and arrested. The rider was assessed by medical staff and determined that he couldn't ride. What a terrible blow to the US team. Tully was upset, and Elaina felt that what happened happened. They had to deal with it and move on.

Now a lot more pressure was on the last riders. Tully changed the lineup. He didn't want April to ride until last to spare her. He felt he would use her in a clutch, and now his options were running out. As the other riders competed, there were little deductions that began to chip away at the US Team's score. Tully began to pace, now he knew he didn't have a choice. He knew April had to ride and hopefully pull this off. He was feeling doubtful.

A groom hoisted April onto Old Roger. She felt him quiver beneath her. Old Roger was ready. April took a big breath and rode up on deck. Germany was finishing, she was next, and Italy was after her. Some of the staff began to talk about her. She heard it and ignored them. She decided to give them something to talk about.

Soon the gate opened, she began a canter with Old Roger. One pass around and they began. They cleared each jump, rounded every pass perfectly. Old Roger still had his shine. They did so amazingly well that the spectators in the stands began to be quiet. Some stood up, so they could watch this young rider. She had poise, was collected, alert, and it as obvious she came to win.

April and Old Rodger were one. Two jumps were twelve feet, and as they approached, April gut kicked Old Rodger to clear it. Rodger understood and he sailed. The only thing that touched that top rail was his soft, feathery tail. The spectators began to clap, which was a real turn on for the hot dog, Old Roger.

Four more jumps and they were clear. April thought, circle wide, two down, and one big jump again. Old Rodger's feet were collected as he gathered speed. April trusted him. She heard his feet and then there was nothing. Nothing but air. And as he landed, it was feet again. The noise in the stadium became loud. Usually, you can't hear it, but April did.

One more jump and they were finished. She touched Old Roger on his neck and whispered. "One more boy. One more." He gathered speed and jumped that last jump like he was jumping a twig.

The crowd erupted into cheers, whistles, and clapping. Tully and Elaina were on the sidelines grimacing as April jumped, then sighing with relief after each one. As they cleared the big jumps Tully felt relief and elation. It was within their reach if she could jump clear without faults. April and Old Roger had captured the crowd, and if you can do that, you've already won. As they floated over the last big jump, Tully knew. He knew they had more than a chance. It was now up to the judges.

As April exited the arena, the crowd was still hollering, whistling, and clapping. Tully and Elaina ran to her. They greeted her slapping her legs and congratulating her. Old Roger was eating up the attention. He saw his first rider at the rail, and walked to him. Artie had tears in his eyes. This horse was almost destroyed seven years ago. Artie thought he had saved Old Roger, but the truth was, it was Old Roger who always saved everyone else. He had the heart of a soldier, a real fighter who never gave in. Artie was grateful that Old Roger was able to shine again. He had earned his press time as well. He was also grateful for this young girl with a heart that matched his Old Roger's. She had a fighting spirit. She didn't back down no matter the odds.

Yes, these two were like a Cinderella story. And the press was going to eat it up and have a field day. Yes, sir. These two would sell a lot of newspapers. The televised version wouldn't come to the United States until nightfall, and Miranda and Gordon wouldn't leave home. They opened their home to those who had helped them. They made meatball hoagies, homemade pierogies, and broccoli salad. They wouldn't miss this for the world.

When the phone rang it was Poppo asking about "her" and how she did. It was a tearful conversation on both ends of the phone.

Poppo put down a wad of money to have a satellite installed so they could "watch television." He said he wouldn't have missed his soulmate ride in the Olympics for all the money in his checkbook. His wife said nothing. She knew how he felt, and she agreed.

Throughout the day, Gordon had his radio on in the cruiser. He heard of a young hero that saved the day for the United States. The announcer didn't say what team, or what event it was, just news would follow. But he had to respond to a call and missed it.

That evening as they gathered in the Di Angelo's home, eleven people were waiting, including the Marshalls, as the Olympic start came on the television. There were rundowns of what TV would cover. In the very beginning, the announcer said there was an upset, the United States was victorious in the equestrian arena by a charismatic young rider and her horse. They all got excited, and Miranda reached for the box of tissues. They all looked at her.

"If I can't be proud of our daughter and cry happy tears, then I don't understand parenthood."

And two women said, "You go ahead and cry. We understand. We will need tissues too!"

The newscaster jumped right into the Olympic news. The US Equestrian Team had indeed won their event. There had been a horrific accident caused by a spectator, when out of the team an angel came. She had her wings on. And there was their daughter, riding that big beautiful horse. They were polished and professional. They televised their entire ride. Gordon's heart jumped with her over those huge twelve-foot jumps. They saw the great horse jump with ease, and only his tail coming down onto the top rail. It was spectacular. What a ride!

Miranda was into her seventh tissue, laughing and crying

together. April had done it. Her daughter had made history. She brought honor and pride to her community and represented the United States with grace. Miranda could never have asked for more.

Gordon's feelings matched his wife's. They were elated that their daughter did so well. For all this time that they missed her, they felt it was worth the effort, and it was. It truly was.

Their friends congratulated both Gordon and Miranda and asked them when April would be coming home.

"They said there should be a parade of some sort for her," said Mrs. Marshall. They didn't know anyone in that town who had been to the Olympics—maybe as a spectator, but never someone who had competed. Someone was going to call the bus service company, and another was to call the mayor of the town. She knew him well enough. She shared a social party with the mayor's wife, and he also bought one of their ponies. Miranda was certain a parade wasn't too much to ask for. Besides being from Fresno, April was now an international star, and stars have great power. Yes, they were all happy, elated!

But soon the winds of change would blow.

Is That Her?

There was another family watching the Olympics that evening, two older teenage boys and their mother. Their chores were done, and they wanted to watch the Olympics that were only on every two years. As the mother watched, she was curious about the young rider.

Could that be her daughter? She looked like her, a bit older, but could it be? No, that couldn't be. That girl was in Germany, but they did say the United States was riding. The mother leaned this way and that to see her face.

As she listened, she learned the rider's name. It was April Di Angelo, and she was from California. The two boys became nervous, wanting to change the channel, and the mother forbade them. She stood to watch the rider and began to cry. It was her. It had to be her. Now she had to contact someone to get her daughter.

Oh, my goodness. What a blessing. What a stroke of luck. Who would have guessed that after such a long time, she would be found, and on television in the Olympics. Thanks be to God above.

Printed in the United States
by Baker & Taylor Publisher Services